C000186814

149

The Proper Care of
COCKATIELS

TW-105

Photography: *Dr. Gerald Allen, Glen Axelrod, Dr. Herbert R. Axelrod, H. Bielfeld, D.K. Blackmore, Rebecca Brega, Dr. E.W. Burr, Ralph Cooper, Michael Defreitas, T.C. Dennett, John P. Donahue, Isabelle Francais, Michael Gilroy, E. Goldfinger, J.E. Grimes, Manolo Guevara, Ray Hanson, M. Heidenreich, Dr. F.W. Huchzermeyer, Ralph Kaehler, B. Kahl, I.F. Keymer, N. Kummerfeld, Bruce D. Lavoy, Horst Müller, William Parlee, Nancy Reed, N. Richmond, Mark Runnals, San Diego Zoo, Brian Seed, Vincent Serbin, Julie Sturman, Tony Tilford, Louise B. Van der Meid, Vogelpark Walsrode, Dr. Matthew Vriends, Wayne Wallace, R. Williams, D.K. Windsor, Jr.*

© Copyright 1992 by T.F.H. Publications, Inc.

Distributed in the UNITED STATES by T.F.H. Publications, Inc., One T.F.H. Plaza, Neptune City, NJ 07753; in CANADA to the Pet Trade by H & L Pet Supplies Inc., 27 Kingston Crescent, Kitchener, Ontario N2B 2T6; Rolf C. Hagen Ltd., 3225 Sartelon Street, Montreal 382 Quebec; in CANADA to the Book Trade by Macmillan of Canada (A Division of Canada Publishing Corporation), 164 Commander Boulevard, Agincourt, Ontario M1S 3C7; in ENGLAND by T.F.H. Publications, PO Box 15, Waterlooville PO7 6BQ; in AUSTRALIA AND THE SOUTH PACIFIC by T.F.H. (Australia) Pty. Ltd., Box 149, Brookvale 2100 N.S.W., Australia; in NEW ZEALAND by Ross Haines & Son, Ltd., 82 D Elizabeth Knox Place, Panmure, Auckland, New Zealand; in the PHILIPPINES by Bio-Research, 5 Lippay Street, San Lorenzo Village, Makati, Rizal; in SOUTH AFRICA by Multipet Pty. Ltd., P.O. Box 35347, Northway, 4065, South Africa. Published by T.F.H. Publications, Inc. Manufactured in the United States of America by T.F.H. Publications, Inc.

The Proper Care of
COCKATIELS

Karl-Herbert Delpy

The Cockatiel's charming temperament is but one reason why these birds are such popular avian pets.

Contents

Preface

The Cockatiel, to whom this little book is devoted, was for many decades cast in the shade by birds of brighter colors, among them most notably the Budgerigar. Frequently the fancier also shied away from acquiring this animal because he feared its size might cause problems.

Apart from the need for a bigger and thus more expensive cage, however, these problems do not exist. Nor is there any reason to be afraid of a slightly larger bird, for the Cockatiel is very amiable. Above all, however, it is by no means more difficult to

Above: This attractive bird makes an ideal aviary bird because it is neither noisy nor destructive.
Opposite: The Cockatiel's amiable behavior makes it a wonderful pet.

Left: *Various mutations have occurred in Cockatiels over the past 30 years.* **Opposite:** *Tame cockatiels can easily be trained to climb various objects such as a chain.*

keep than a Budgerigar.

For these reasons, I have been only too pleased to comply with the publisher's request to write the monograph upon this bird that was still missing from their extensive range of special literature. It has been done in the hope of winning new friends for this charming Australian.

This small volume is intended primarily for bird fanciers who have

Today commercial seed mixtures often contain, in addition to seeds, dietary supplements designed to make the mixture a better balanced diet.

acquired this type of pet for the very first time. If you follow the advice I have compiled in these pages in as much detail as possible, your animal will be as well cared for as would be desirable with respect to all household pets under human care. I would also like to think, however, that more experienced fanciers, too, will turn the leaves of this new publication with interest.

The New Member of Your Household

Isn't it a beautiful bird? Certainly, there are more brightly-colored birds on our planet, but its pale-gray basic color, contrasting with the white feathers of the wings, in

It is important to read all the information you can about your new pet so you will understand what it needs to grow into a healthy mature Cockatiel.

Notice the differences in feather colors of these Pearl Pied Cockatiels.

combination with the lemon-yellow cheeks and the orange-colored ear coverts, is always a pleasant sight.

This bird has genuine charm. When it cocks its head to one side, with the pretty crest erect, and looks at you inquiringly with its big brown eyes, you will

Although other birds have more colorful bodies and plumage, the Cockatiel is, nonetheless, a very beautiful bird.

Note the inquisitive expression of this Cockatiel. The Cockatiel, in fact, is a very bright, perceptive bird.

not deny it your friendship and admiration.

As is common in nature, the male Cockatiel is the more handsome sex. He is not only larger in stature and of a stronger build than the female but more vivid in color as well. In the hen, the yellow and orange plumage colors are quite faint. The latter, incidentally, applies to juveniles as well, generally speaking.

The correct length of a fully grown Cockatiel with no degeneration due to inbreeding is about 29 to 33 cm. Slightly less than half of this falls to the share of the tail.

The colors of a male Cockatiel tend to be more brilliant than that of the female. The male is also larger in build than the female.

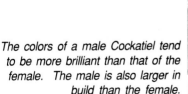

The voice of the Cockatiel corresponds in volume to its body size. This probably makes the bird a less suitable companion for people who like peace and quiet. The shrill notes it utters in sudden fright or when anything unusual is happening are by no means the rule, however. After the necessary acclimatization it will be heard less frequently. As with all

Even a sharply screeching Cockatiel will normally calm down once it has become familiar with its new surroundings.

Like most other birds, the Cockatiel is constantly preening, or grooming, its feathers.

parrot species, there is some risk that the Cockatiel one has bought may turn out to be a constant noise-maker that has been ruined by the wrong treatment during its juvenile stage. For this reason, it is advisable to unobtrusively observe the bird over a period of time before making the purchase.

Note the four-toed feet, with two prehensile toes pointing forward and two

The Cockatiel's acrobatic feats make it an entertaining and enjoyable pet.

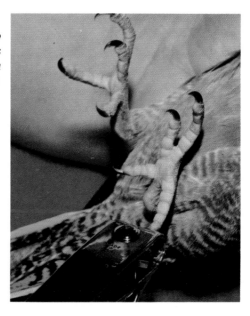

The interesting structure of the Cockatiel's toes enables the bird to be a very agile climber.

pointing in the opposite direction. This arrangement of the toes is the special characteristic of birds who are very agile climbers, and it allows the Cockatiel to perform proper gymnastic feats which are a constant delight to its keeper.

Where does the Cockatiel come from?

The Cockatiel
  Genus: *Nymphicus*
(not *Kakadus!*)
  Sole species:
Nymphicus hollandicus
(Kerr)

Our Cockatiel originates from a distant land which also happens to be the smallest continent on earth. The geographical

Opposite: *This two-year-old female, "Bonnie," is a Normal female, not a mutation, as evidenced by the typical gray feathers on the breast and wings.* ***Below:*** *The Cockatiel,* Nymphicus hollandicus, *originated in the continent of Australia.*

The threat display is very similar to the position that is assumed when bathing in the rain. All the flight feathers are extended to expose a maximum area to the falling moisture.

isolation from the rest of the world has resulted in a particularly varied fauna there. Among the four continents to which parrots are native, Australia is the home of the most beautiful specimens

and the greatest abundance of species and, consequently, has been the frequently visited destination of many renowned ornithologists. Australian large parakeets have for many years ranked among the absolute

The Cockatiel does not exhibit the nasty temperament that is characteristic of some other birds.

favorites in fanciers' hands. While the Cockatoos, which also originate from Australia, were well-known and popular in classical antiquity for being decorative, readily tamed, and for easily learning to talk, they have fallen out of favor in modern times because of their noisy screaming. The Cockatiel bears a considerable resemblance to the smaller Cockatoos in many respects but fortunately lacks their violent temperament, their destructive gnawing, and certain of their other unpleasant bad habits. Despite the aforementioned

Left: The Cockatiel has become quite a favorite among those who keep birds as pets.
Opposite: The Cockatiel and the small Cockatoos have many physical similarities.

resemblance the Cockatiel continues to be regarded as an independent species without close relatives, i.e., as the product of parallel evolution. This theory is supported by the fact that its behavior is indeed of a fundamentally different nature. Furthermore, the Cockatiel lacks the versatility of the true Cockatoos when it comes to moving the crest.

As is well known, subsequent to its discovery, Australia was for a long time part of the British Empire as a penal colony. It is likely that deported

Above: The Cockatiel is considered an independent species without any close relatives. **Opposite:** Parents remain near the nest entrance at all times.

criminals were the first who had the chance to admire the flights of this magnificent bird in its natural habitat. Its first description and classification we owe to a man named Gmelin, and this goes back to the end of the 18th century.

Today the Cockatiel is still found in large numbers in the coastal regions of Australia. Unlike the Budgerigars, which also originate from there, it is not seen in large flights but more commonly moves

Most likely, British criminals deported to Australia were the first Europeans to see the Cockatiel.

Cockatiels prefer moving around in small groups rather than in large flocks.

about the countryside nomadically, in search of food, in groups of up to 20 individuals.

Its discovery for the fanciers in Europe at the beginning of the 19th century coincided with a highly progressive phase in the history of ornithology and a constant supply of new imports in such numbers as were never reached again. The famous British ornithologist John Gould (1804-1881), author of numerous books on Australian birds, which were published between 1837 and 1865 and have remained unsurpassed to this day, also provides several reports on the Cockatiel.

Imports of Australian birds into Europe reached such proportions at that time that as early as 1894 the government of that country imposed the

Mutual preening, sometimes referred to as allopreening, is usually focused on the head region.

Left: *Many of the first Cockatiels brought to Britain in the 18th century could not survive the climate differences between Australia and Britain.* **Opposite:** *Successful captive breeding did not occur until the latter part of the 19th century.*

first export embargo. It is well known that the Australian colonists found Parakeets and Cockatoos to be harvest pests which occur in flights and destroyed them on a massive scale by disseminating poison at the relatively few watering places. The losses caused in this way are certain to have been as serious as the adverse consequences of export,

if not even more so.

A few individual Cockatiels had reached Great Britain at the beginning of the 19th century. They were brought back by mariners who took these birds aboard their sailing vessels with them on the journeys, which lasted for months. In the damp, cold British climate such animals that had been alive on arrival very soon died. Reports of successful breeding in captivity did not begin to appear in any great numbers until around 1860 at the earliest.

There has never been

This baby Cockatiel has just emerged from the nest hollow and will soon attempt its first flight.

In the wild, young Cockatiels are fed principally on ripening grass seeds.

any serious danger of the Cockatiel becoming extinct in Australia. It is worth mentioning that this bird is frequently seen on the ground in its natural environment, too. If its breeding season in Australia falls into the period from October to December, this is connected purely with the high number of rainfalls at the onset of the rainy season. These make the wild grasses grow very tall and their seeds, when ripened, provide the huge quantities of rearing food which are needed once the young have hatched.

Today the Cockatiel is not only well-known in nearly every country on earth but is also

being bred in captivity with great success all the year 'round. For this reason, the prices that are being asked for an exotic bird of this size have become comparatively modest.

Today, only birds which were bred locally and have fully adapted to the local climate and to life in captivity are for sale to members of the general public.

Another factor in the Cockatiel's popularity is its success in being bred in captivity.

Correct Accommodation

The selection of a suitable cage for keeping a Cockatiel is of far greater importance than the layman is likely to suppose. If a bird of the size of a pigeon is to be cared for in one's home, it must be realized that mini-sized cages are out of the question on account of their small size alone. What is

Be sure to purchase a cage that provides your bird enough room to move around.

needed instead is a bird-cage which enables the new pet to turn around without coming into contact with the bars and which also allows it to spread out its wings when it wants to. The bird-cage should not be

Below: Unless you have a special reason for not having one, the cage should always have a wooden perch. ***Opposite:*** Many cages are designed as decorator items for the household.

selected primarily for its pleasing appearance or as something that fits in with the furniture and the interior decorations. It is more appropriate to give all due consideration to the requirements of your new friend first.

Unfortunately the choice of special cages is not an overwhelming one. Round models or those designed like Japanese tea-houses, with recesses, balconies, decorations, turrets, etc. completely

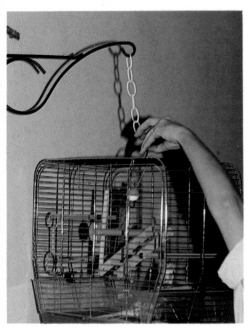

If you have young children or pets that might hurt the bird, consider having the cage out of their reach.

Cages with few or no horizontal wires should be avoided. They make it difficult, if not impossible, for the Cockatiel to climb up the sides, which is one of their favorite pastimes.

Top: *Setting up the cage in advance means that you will not have to disturb the new Cockatiel once it's put in.* ***Above:*** *Bird gravel, also called sand or grit, can be used to cover the floor of the cage.*

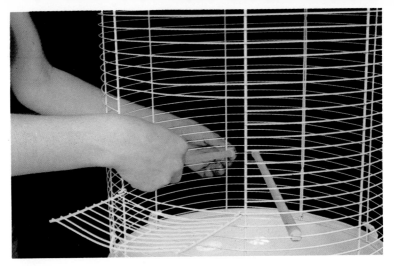

Top: Perches should be placed where they offer easy access to food and water. **Above:** The small-seed mix is offered in its own dish.

fail to impress the inmate. Flight cages with a chrome finish, for Budgerigars and exotic birds, about 60 cm long, 40 cm high, and 35 cm deep, are best suited to the size and habits of the Cockatiel. Cages with wooden frames, the so-called beechwood cages, are of use only as a temporary measure. Apart from being more difficult to clean, they would not stand up to the Cockatiel's sharp beak without getting damaged.

Plastic dishes and pull-out trays have become standard equipment in modern cage designs. They reduce the scattering of seeds, husks, and sand to a minimum. Since the rows of perches all tend to be identical in diameter, you would be doing your bird a favor if you replaced one or two of them with thicker ones straightaway.

Incidentally, a bird of that size should be able to make do with four perches, thus ensuring it has enough room to move about in. It

Cockatiels enjoy a variety of foods in their dishes, including different types of seeds.

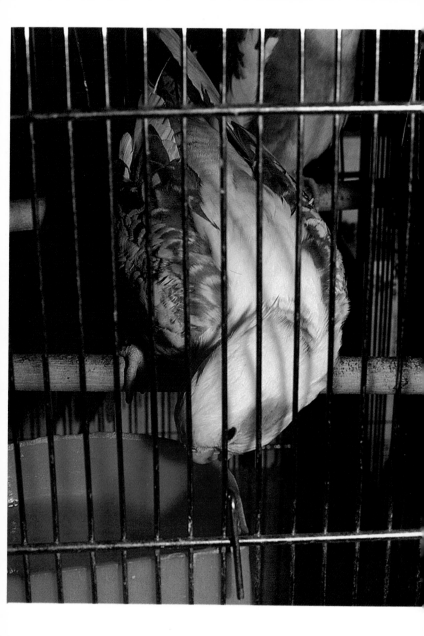

Opposite: Change the bird's water daily; the seed dish should be cleaned at least twice a week. Right: Birds enjoy spray millet so much it is almost as much a toy as a food. Below: Cockatiels are playful enough to enjoy having one or two toys in the cage.

is a very common mistake to clutter up the cage with an excess number of perches, swings, ladders, and toys.

Now just a quick word about the "dirt-grid" fitted in some cages for Parrots quite a few centimeters above the bottom of the pull-out tray that goes with it. I regard such grids not only as unnatural but also, in the long term, as injurious to the bird's health. All

In aviaries, it is preferable to fashion the opening of the nest log in the form of a canopy, which will give maximum protection if it rains. Alternatively the nest log can be placed under a shelter.

Cockatiels will not use the kind of nesting matrials made available for other birds, as their nest construction is simple, amounting to a depression in the floor of the nesting chamber.

birds would obviously much prefer to sit on a smooth surface or a soft one. Furthermore, the express purpose of putting a mixture of bird-sand and lime, grit, etc. into the cage is to ensure that the birds are able to ingest these substances, which significantly aid digestion. Although it is possible to keep a Cockatiel on a post or climbing-tree, just like other Parrots, it is not advisable to dispense with a cage altogether. On the other hand, the

fancier who wishes to provide this type of equipment for use during the hours of free flight inside the house certainly does the animal a big favor.

Left: More than one kind of food can be placed in the cage at a time. **Above:** Another type of rope toy that the Cockatiel can play with.

The Best Location for the Bird-home

In this respect, ignorance is responsible for a great deal of problems. First of all, it is essential to decide on a permanent site. Birds which are constantly being moved about inside the house are to be pitied. Totally unsuitable are drafty places or, if the windows are facing south, locations which routinely get the full glare of the sun. Dark corners are equally unsuited. As for the top of the kitchen cabinet so popular with some bird fanciers, this is

Opposite: Do not move your bird around from place to place. Let it become familiar with its surroundings. **Above:** Be sure your pet is not exposed to poisonous plants.

positively dangerous for cage birds.

As an animal-lover, you should always remember that your pet lacks the freedom to choose where it wants to be as it has in its natural environment. Wherever you place the cage the bird has to put up with what turns out to be its lot: cooking and frying fumes, leaking gas, great heat, or tobacco smoke when the cage is placed too high up, for example. One case became known where in quick succession several birds died of asphyxia caused by fumes from hot fat. On the top of the kitchen cabinet in question, immediately below the ceiling, temperatures of up to 35°C prevailed in the winter. When the kitchen needed airing the temperature dropped to 15°C for a brief period. No living creature is able to tolerate such conditions! Sudden drops in temperature in rooms which, for whatever reason, require to be aired thoroughly several times a day can thus be the cause of not a few "inexplicable" mortalities. As well, many birds whose owners believe they are giving them the best possible care are killed

Opposite: Be sure to have consideration for your new pet and provide it with the proper surroundings. Maintaining an even, moderate temperature is vital for the Cockatiel's well-being.

Above: *A pair of Cockatiels in a normal cage with a few rungs cut out to accommodate a nesting box.* **Opposite:** *Improper care and maintenance are the cause of many "inexplicable" fatalities.*

by the full glare of the sun in the summer, or by a constant supply of cold air in the winter. In these cases the cage is located in the window and it is hoped that at least the window frames have a tight fit. Strictly

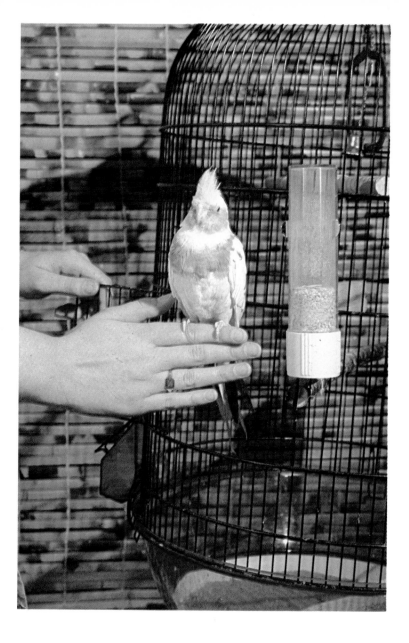

speaking, the kitchen should never be chosen as a location for bird cages.

The temperatures which normally prevail wherever the pet keeper would like the cage to be located can quickly be established by means of a thermometer. Whether there is a constant draft in this spot will be revealed by a flickering candle.

On the other hand, the belief that the proximity of a television set endangers the lives of all cage birds has long been proved wrong. The amount of radiation emitted by the tube is so slight that even a smaller bird comes to no harm. The only real drawback is

that the flickering of the TV screen strains the bird's eyes, which

Tobacco smoke can cause serious health problems for your Cockatiel. These problems can be as extreme as death by asphyxiation from rising tobacco smoke.

Above: *Be sure that your cage is a suitable size for the number of birds you have.* ***Opposite:*** *Large areas may be fenced in to provide your Cockatiels with more room to fly while remaining confined.*

could eventually result in mild conjunctivitis. This risk can readily be eliminated by covering the cage with a cloth.

The animal lover who, although feeling concerned for his pet, switches on his television set by means of an ultrasound remote control should bear in mind that these sound waves are

perceived as distressing in the more sensitive auditory canal of domestic animals. On the other hand, they cause the distress only when the domestic animal happens to be somewhere between the transmitter and the receiving set, i.e., in our case if the cage were to be so placed. More thorough investigations have so far not been carried out.

Be aware of what your Cockatiel needs to have a happy and healthy existence in your household.

Consideration Towards the Cockatiel

Most people who keep animals are prepared to show consideration towards them. The domestic pet is entirely at the mercy of its keeper and totally dependent on him. While the Cockatiel seldom comes to any harm inside its closed cage, the dangers that threaten it during its free flight in the room are considerable.

The bird who comes tripping after its keeper can easily be trodden on or caught in a door. The animal

It is up to the bird's keeper to watch out for its safety in the house.

The kitchen area offers several potential hazards and should therefore be off limits to your Cockatiel.

is not aware, either, that some houseplants are poisonous to it and upset its tummy.

Since a bird is unable to recognize glass, it flies through windowpanes which are not protected by net curtains and dies instantly or breaks its neck or suffers some form of paralysis due to effusions of blood in the brain.

Birds that fly above escaping steam often end up inside the

stock-pot. Hot radiators, hot kitchen stoves, or electric heaters which have just been switched off are regarded as convenient perches by the small animal. Even if it has burned its feet on them once before, it rarely learns from this unpleasant experience. These are the things the bird keeper has to

You may have houseplants that are poisonous to the Cockatiel and will make it extremely ill.

The Cockatiel's keeper must be sure to make the surroundings safe and pleasant for the bird.

think of.

Items about cage birds that have escaped into dangerous freedom through doors or windows which were left open, particularly on hot summer days, appear in the columns of our daily newspapers with unfailing regularity. Where a large crowd of people sit in the same room

Remember, an open window is an open invitation for your Cockatiel to leave your household.

This six-week-old Cockatiel is only beginning to learn of the dangers it may face in the domestic setting.

and the tobacco-smoke below the ceiling is getting thicker, no bird can feel comfortable. The same applies if it is in front of and close to the television screen and the set is switched on for hours on end.

The drastic changes in temperature which can endanger the Cockatiel's life include taking the bird from a heated room into an unheated one. If in doubt, opt for whatever constitutes the lesser risk. Beware of putting animals that are normally kept in a warm environment into an outdoor flight during the cool months of the year.

Cages standing in the full glare of the sun have been known to cause their inmates to suffer fatal heat-strokes even if the birds originated from tropical zones. It is essential, therefore, to treat a

Make sure that the cage's permanent place suits the needs of the Cockatiel. It must be in an area of a consistently moderate temperature, and away from direct sunlight.

bird with as much consideration as one would extend to a dog. Since it is a fact that the majority of all mortalities in cage birds can be traced back to unsuitable cage sites or a lack of regard for the bird's requirements, it seemed advisable to deal with these topics in some detail here.

Diet

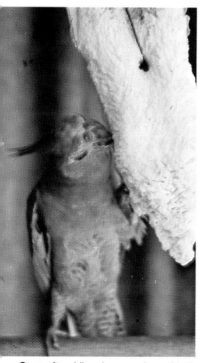

Opposite: Vitamins can be added to the Cockatiel's drinking water; however, one should administer vitamins by hand to a sick bird.
Above: Cuttlebone is an essential ingredient in the Cockatiel's diet.

Let me say from the outset that the Cockatiel, being a seed-eater, is very undemanding where its diet is concerned. In the long term, however, you are not doing your bird a favor if you carefully observe what seeds get picked out of the normal commercial mix first and then never buy anything other than, for instance, hemp and sunflower seeds. A monotonous diet is harmful to all living creatures. Ready-mixed seeds for Cockatiels can be purchased, both loose and in packets. To make a statement that one mix is better than another is no longer true. You will observe, however, that Cockatiels in particular develop a genuinely individual taste. It may be that your bird avoids the seeds which your neighbor's bird consumes with relish.

A simple recipe for preparing a suitable Cockatiel mix of your own is to add 200 g of light or dark sunflower seeds and 50 g of hemp

Not all Cockatiels enjoy the same food in their diet. It is important to find out quickly what kind of foods your Cockatiel prefers.

Cockatiels are fond of chewing on leaves, twigs, and bark. These items should be supplied regularly.

to 500 g of standard Budgerigar mix (or one large packet of Budgerigar mix). If you learn through careful observation what seeds your bird is particularly partial to, you will soon be able to offer a varied diet on which your pet will thrive.

Hemp and sunflower seeds, although greatly liked by most

Sunflower seeds are another delicacy that most Cockatiels enjoy having in their diet.

Cockatiels, have a very high fat content. Unless the bird gets more than an above average amount of exercise which enables it to use up the excess calories, it will quickly get fat.

Suitable as foods are all the different varieties of millet, oats, groats, germinated oat grains, Canary seed, sunflower seeds of all colors, and good hemp in small quantities. In addition, stalks of the well-known spray millet, rusks or commercial wafers, chew-sticks with millet, and once a week one slice of hard-boiled egg; the white and the yolk of egg

Green food is a good supplement to your bird's diet as long as its digestive tract remains in good working order. If problems such as diarrhea set in, greens should be taken out of the bird's food supply.

should be offered. As a supplement in the form of fruit, sweet apples or firm pears are most readily digestible.

The use of green food as a dietary supplement is a more difficult problem. Although beneficial and a good source of vitamins where the digestion is normal, it must be withheld at once if there is an onset of diarrhea; the same applies where fruit is concerned. When choosing green food most people immediately select ordinary lettuce without considering that it consists of 95% water, has almost invariably been sprayed with pesticides, and, if it comes out of the hothouse, does not contain any significant amounts of vitamins. Over and above that, it spoils very rapidly. Endive lettuce (green leaves, please!) and the well-known wild dandelion are far better suited as vitamin supplements with regard to cage birds. That green food of any kind should be washed before it is given to the birds goes without saying. It becomes dangerous, however,

Opposite: Typically, the mixture used for hand-rearing chicks has the same cereal basis as the staple diet of adult Cockatiels.

when offered to them dripping-wet. Carrots, which have the additional advantage of satisfying the birds' gnawing needs, are very valuable and always harmless. The fancier who wants to give special consideration to this innate characteristic of the Cockatiels should put sections of branches from healthy, unsprayed fruit trees into the cage. Suitable supplements from the vegetable garden consist of spinach and silver beet.

Chickweed—not usually known to most consumers—is the healthiest green food.

In addition to bird-sand, the bottom of the cage should also be covered with a mixture of pigeon grit, crushed lime, sea-shells, and gravel. Complete mineral mixes such as can be purchased for

Foods meant for human consumption are just that. They are not meant to be for your Cockatiel and may cause illness or other problems.

pigeons, are acceptable. The bottom of the cage is to be kept clean and free from dietary supplements at all times; it should be noted that the white cuttlebone derived from the cuttlefish can withstand the strong beak for only a very short time. Crushed egg-shells, widely used in the past when nothing else was available, can no longer be recommended since they tempt breeding birds into devouring their own eggs. Moreover, they transmit many bacteria, including the dangerous *Salmonellae*.

Bird fanciers often take special pride in

being able to relate that their pet loves sausages and cheese, is passionately fond of beer or spirits, or regards coffee as a great treat. Also, that the animal likes helping itself to butter and other foods meant for human consumption. This is regarded as "cute." The tame bird with a fondness for alcohol has its praises sung for being "a great character" and "absolutely unique." Since the digestive system of a bird is not really able to cope with foods intended for other species, the inevitable consequence of this (unfortunately still widespread) foolish behavior on the owner's part is that the animal

Below: Two types of Cockatiel mix that can be used to provide needed vitamins and nutrients to your bird. *Opposite:* Two Cockatiels enjoying a large chunk of cuttlebone.

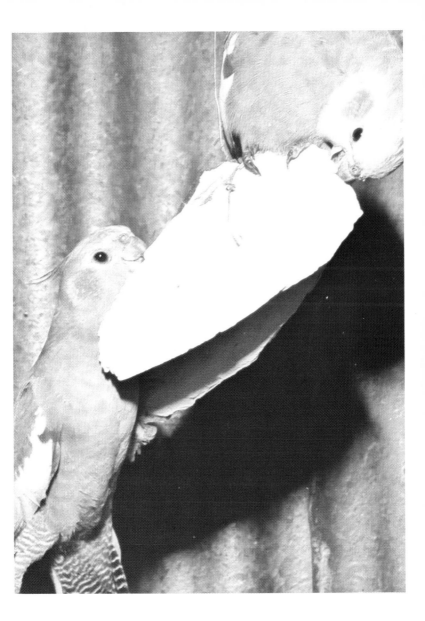

Above: *A food hopper, like the one shown here, is better than an open dish because the bird cannot scatter its food about the floor by standing in it.*
Opposite: *With Cockatiel chicks, food from a spoon most closely approximates feeding from the bill of a parent bird.*

becomes ill or dies prematurely. Alcohol and hot spices are particularly harmful.

The most common long term effect, apart from chronic molt and straggly-looking plumage, which tend to get blamed for anything but what actually caused them, is cirrhosis of the liver. Experts and animal lovers alike shudder when having to listen to such tales.

Chemical products—whether intended to improve plumage color,

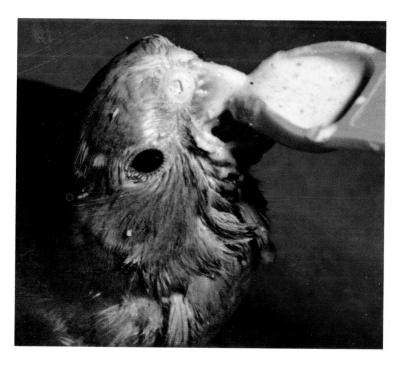

to depress or increase the sex drive, or to improve fertility, etc.— are of very limited value in bird keeping, the only exception being parasiticides.

The food should be supplied at roughly the same time every day. Contrary to the widespread opinion of inexperienced bird fanciers, no parrot will stuff itself to bursting point at the first

In the wild, Cockatiels feed mostly on seeds found on the ground.

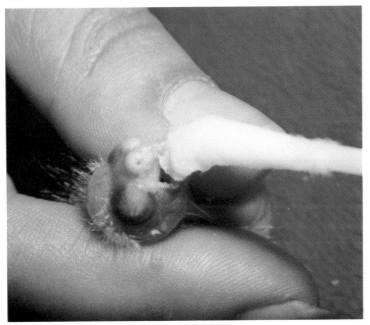

With very young chicks, gently wash the chick's face after each feeding session, especially in and around the mouth, with a cotton swab moistened with warm water.

opportunity. It is not necessary, therefore, to administer the food by the spoonful or in careful rations. The dish should always be filled to just below the brim. The keeper removes the husks in the dish by blowing them away. Many a cage bird has been known to die of starvation in front of a seed dish containing nothing but husks because the keeper was under the mistaken impression that the bird still had plenty of food.

Unlike domestic hens and pigeons, the Cockatiel does not swallow the seeds whole. It shells them with its beak and eats only the inner grain. Another fairly widespread erroneous idea is that water must be boiled before it is given. Boiled water is flavorless and without life. It is of no nutritional value and is

Bird seed blocks come in several different styles and shapes and may contain different kinds of seeds.

Unlike many other birds, the Cockatiel breaks food up in its mouth before finally swallowing it.

justified only in cases of intestinal disorders and even then only for a few days. Nor should drinking water for birds be administered ice cold or straight from the tap. Otherwise, it should be as fresh as possible and in the summer it should be replaced several times a day.

The owner who plans to be away for more than a day should note

the following: Because the metabolic rate of birds is higher than that of mammals, even a large bird like the Cockatiel can die of starvation very quickly. If the seed dish is empty, the bird's fat deposits are used up within a period of a few hours. They are replaced equally rapidly, of course. On the other hand, where no water is supplied a bird originating from the dry Australian grassy steppes, it can manage for several days, if necessary, without risk to its life.

Here an adult Cockatiel is feeding a chick. As the food is swallowed the chick jerks its head rapidly up and down.

Maintenance

At least twice a week the cage tray should be pulled out and its bottom, after having been cleaned, covered with a layer of prepared bird sand, about 1 cm deep. The Cockatiel is decidedly unlikely to have any objections to having its confined living space freshened up every so often.

It is advantageous to wash the cage every other week with warm water to which a liquid cleansing agent for normal domestic use has been added. In the past, boiling water was used, or the whole cage was put into the oven to prevent an infestation with insects. Modern cage materials would not withstand such treatment. In the rare event of parasites occurring, more appropriate remedies are available which are applied to the cage with a brush or sprinkled onto it without the

Opposite: Be sure to clean your Cockatiel's cage on a regular basis. This will not only keep it looking nice but also will help prevent the growth of harmful bacteria and other undesirable elements in the cage.

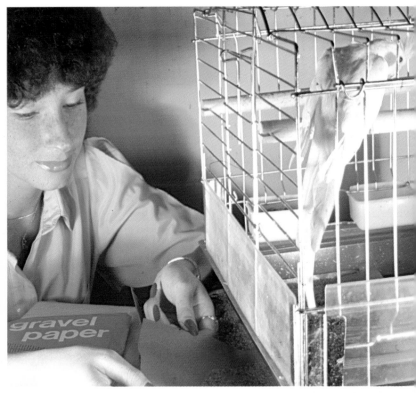

Above: *The cage tray should be taken out and cleaned approximately twice a week. A fresh sheet of gravel paper should be placed on the bottom of the tray.* **Opposite:** *Once the gravel paper is set, place a new layer of prepared bird sand about 1 cm thick in the tray.*

whole procedure degenerating into hard work.

The often voiced opinion that a bird that is left on its own all day invariably ends up deteriorating is a myth. On the other hand, it goes without saying that no pet should be left to its own devices for days on end.

Whether or not the

bird cage should be covered with a cloth at night remains a matter for controversy among bird fanciers. Experts rightly regard it as unnatural. The method undoubtedly has its advantages, however, if it protects the animal from drafts, bright light, or constant disturbances during the normal sleeping

period. Experience has shown that in most families this type of situation arises at weekends when there are guests in the house and people go to bed later than usual.

I would like to point out that refrigerators which start noisily and with vibrations at regular intervals are unsuitable as cage sites as are domestic washing machines. The immediate vicinity of a frequently ringing telephone, or of record players, radios, and

Cockatiels drink extensively during the typical day. Always be sure to have enough of a water supply for your bird. Plant saucers, like the one shown here, fill the requirements of a water dish.

In this photo the male is regurgitating food from the crop and prepares to feed his begging offspring.

television sets which are switched on late into the night has adverse effects. Even robust creatures like the Cockatiel are sensitive and need a good night's sleep with as little disturbance as possible. A pet bird one would like to grow tame must be carefully protected from constantly recurring shrill noises and from anything which repeatedly causes it to panic.

About Free Flight

The majority of bird fanciers can hardly wait to let their pet out of the cage for free flight inside the room. This means that sooner or later, despite the best of intentions, most pet birds come to some sort of harm. It is a very serious mistake to let a newly purchased bird out of its cage before six weeks have

In large indoor areas, protective wire mesh can be placed over the window to prevent the Cockatiel from flying into the window.

elapsed—before the bird has become used to its new cage and has had ample opportunity to study the new environment and have it imprinted on its memory.

Although I consider it my duty to keep pointing this out, in practice, only a minority of people who buy birds abide by this rule. The majority will want to retort that even the most attractive cage is rather small and therefore the bird is just waiting to get out

Above: The keeper must give the Cockatiel ample time to become familiar with its new surroundings before letting it out for free flight.
Opposite: Birds just out of the nest are usually clumsy fliers, and the wing beats are somewhat slow and labored compared with adults.

Once the Cockatiel has had a chance to take in its surroundings from within the cage, the bird must leave the cage on its own. It must be given an opportunity to slowly familiarize itself with the new environment.

of it as often and as quickly as it can. This is the usual common error of assuming that animals think like human beings! I am not disputing that it can only benefit a cage bird if it is able to use its wings unhindered inside a room occasionally. In cases of circulatory trouble or where there is a risk of overweight, this can save the bird's life. But first the Cockatiel has to become so familiar with the still very cramped space that it does not fly into walls, windows, or furniture,

as compared with the
boundaries of its
natural environment.
The animal learns this
only by leaving the cage
entirely on its own
accord and gradually
exploring the
surroundings with
which it has roughly

familiarized itself from within the cage.

All the fundamental principles of bird keeping are diminished if a pet bird is forced to leave its cage and then,

with the aid of several members of the family or of a broom, in attempts to recapture it, a lifelong fear of human beings is implanted in the animal. That a heavy bird when being chased about like that collides with hard walls, windowpanes, or other objects is virtually inevitable; the frequent outcome is broken wings, if not instant death resulting from a broken neck or a fractured skull. Lasting paralysis due to effusions of blood in the brain cannot be ruled out either. It is so easy to prevent at least the collision with panes of glass by closing the curtains.

If more bird fanciers

Above: Chasing the Cockatiel around in order to recapture it may cause a permanent aversion to human beings. During the chase, the bird will most likely run into objects about the room, possibly causing serious damage to the bird. **Opposite:** The bird must be allowed to leave the cage of its own choice. Forcing the Cockatiel to leave its cage will do nothing but make the bird fear its keeper.

would remember to close the doors and windows **before** letting their pet out of the cage, fewer birds would escape to the outdoors. Often the protest is that the window had been open only a tiny fraction; birds are frequently able to detect these cracks by the current of air.

After having taken all the necessary precautionary measures you let your Cockatiel out of the cage for its free flight, I must point out that this freedom can have disadvantages for the interior decorations. Fine curtains are particularly prone to suffer. Holes gnawed into wallpaper and walls are perhaps less upsetting in the long run. Plant lovers among the bird fanciers are well advised not to

Make sure all windows are completely shut before permitting the Cockatiel to leave the cage.

leave valuable potted plants, rubber plants, and Philodendron in the same room which is to serve as a temporary playground for the Cockatiel. Sometimes the plants become unrecognizable. Free-flying cage birds should never be left without supervision, although it often happens.

If you ever do have the bad luck that your pet escapes from the house, it is generally pointless to try and recapture it in daylight. If at all possible, appoint a member of the family to follow the bird and keep an eye on it through binoculars. Only at dusk will you succeed in catching it. Blinded by torchlight, the animal can be grabbed. It is then carried home inside a bag.

Whatever happens, do not torture yourself with the thought that the escaped Cockatiel is inevitably condemned to death. This widespread opinion is erroneous. At worst, it may apply in severely cold weather and when there is snow. Otherwise only cats and birds of prey can endanger it. From spring to fall, when greenstuff, fruit, and half ripened grass seeds are available in abundance, the bird

Opposite: Trimming the large feathers of the wings will impede flight and lessen the danger of the Cockatiel escaping.

may actually be able to hold its own for months. By supplying food every day one can ensure that the animal gets used to one particular spot and later it can be recaptured there. To have the cage standing nearby will be helpful in that respect.

If no amount of precautions have averted disaster and the escapee has vanished without trace, it is well worthwhile in larger towns to put a "Lost" advertisement into the local paper. Cockatiels at liberty are particularly conspicuous on account of the crest

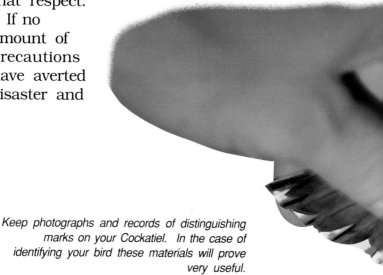

Keep photographs and records of distinguishing marks on your Cockatiel. In the case of identifying your bird these materials will prove very useful.

and the color of the head. Many advertisements have been successful in the past. It is, of course, very useful if you can support your claim to ownership by a knowledge of the ring-number or by means of good photographs, since often it is not the finder who volunteers the decisive information.

Many a bird fancier boasts that having the cage on the windowsill enables the bird to flirt with free living wild

birds and that for a parakeet kept on its own this does much for its distraction and constant entertainment. This opinion is not correct. The activity of the birds it cannot get to causes the caged bird to scream and the noise is then condemned by the owner as a bad habit. Furthermore, the birds the Cockatiel can see from the windowsill are mostly sparrows. Their chirping is easy for the Cockatiel to learn. In the summer the sparrows pass some of their parasites on to the latter.

Grooming, Luxury or Necessity?

Both for human beings and the pets who live with them, grooming is essential and far from superfluous. Most important of all is the bath. Cockatiels are not naturally inclined to have a bath very often since water is very scarce in the grassy steppes where they originate. In the

Above: A Cockatiel grooming and caring for its own feathers. This process is called preening. **Opposite:** Clipping your Cockatiel's feathers is a very delicate operation and should be left for more experienced keepers.

course of their domestication, however, i.e., since being used as household pets and for breeding in large cages and aviaries for more than a thousand years, this dislike of water has become less intense. How stubbornly habits that have been passed on for generations are preserved even after transplanting to another continent and different living conditions is demonstrated by the fervor with which many tame Cockatiels relish a bowl of freshly washed lettuce. This is exactly what they did in Australia, albeit among grasses wet with dew early in the morning.

Many Cockatiels bred in captivity can be acclimatized to a health and beauty bath. Bath houses of the required size are difficult to find, however. Where the bird is granted free flight at regular intervals an existing water tap should be left slightly dripping and the animal will soon make use of that. A plastic basin filled with tepid water, about 1 cm deep, serves the same purpose. The container chosen must be big

Opposite: Much like wing clipping, cutting your Cockatiel's claws is also a delicate process and should be left for someone more experienced. If you decide to cut them, be very careful. When claws are cut too close, bleeding and severe irritation may occur.

Left: *Preening seems to be an instinctive behavior. The youngsters devote long periods to this activity as soon as they emerge from the nest area.* **Opposite:** *In the process of preening the Cockatiels first use the gland at the base of the tail to get the oil from which they groom themselves.*

enough, of course, and above all it must be stable. Once the bird has toppled over with its bath it will never give it another try.

Do not lose patience if your endeavors are not appreciated as much as you had hoped. Parrots, particularly from the Budgerigar to the Ara, are especially fond of being sprayed slowly from above with tepid water in imitation of tropical rain. Hence a simple flower spray best meets the bird's natural requirements, provided the animal does not get soaked to the skin. Only the top layer of the plumage should become wet, which encourages preening and is extremely beneficial both with regard to your pet's good looks and its health. Animals must never be forced into the water!

The constant flying about, running on the ground, and perching on a vast variety of surfaces ensures that the claws of wild birds are kept short naturally. In cage birds, on the other hand, they often grow so excessively long that the animals are severely restricted in their movements.

Accessories such as emery paper covers for the

perches, supposed to save trimming the claws, have not proved effective. Better and at least not harmful to the bird are the ceramic covers (already patented) which are pushed over the perches. These covers are rough only in those areas where the claws grip and not where the toe pads rest. Only two perches should be thus equipped, however, so that the bird has a choice as to the type of perch it wants to sit on.

If trimming is unavoidable, a strong pair of clippers is required. To cut the claw, the latter is held

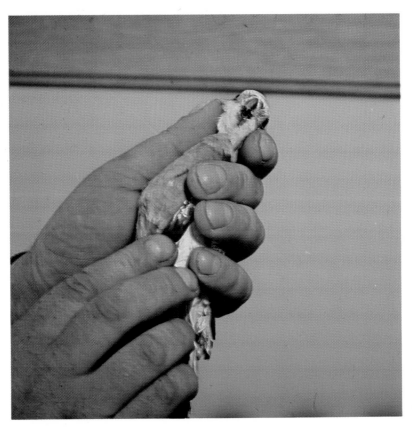

Above: *A good method of holding your Cockatiel while clipping claws and performing other forms of grooming.* **Opposite:** *A Cockatiel in the process of having its wings clipped.*

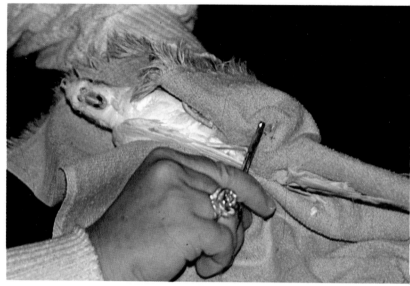

Above: Put the claws in strong light in order to disinguish the blood vessel. This way, the keeper is less likely to cut into the blood vessel and cause bleeding. *Opposite:* Mutual preening is a social activity that occurs normally during mating season.

against a powerful source of light so that the course of the red blood vessel can be clearly discerned through the yellowish horny substance. Where the blood vessel cannot be distinguished, claw trimming is purely a matter of intuition and experience and not for the layman. The extreme limit for trimming is a distance of 1 mm from the onset of the blood vessel.

Claws that have been cut too short bleed copiously. They cause the bird as much pain as you feel when one of your nails has been cut too short or got torn. If the worst has happened, arrest the bleeding under the cold tap, with saliva, or by means of a hemostyptic stick.

Just as an above average growth of the claws frequently occurs only at an advanced age, so an excessively long upper mandible is a relatively common phenomenon in older Cockatiels. Trimming becomes strictly necessary only when the animal is finding it difficult to eat. It also has the disadvantage of stimulating growth. Once one has started trimming, therefore, it will become necessary again every few weeks. No amount of "whetstones" hung up inside the cage make any difference. This does not mean the latter serve no useful purpose at all, however. Like all mineral mixes, they contain calcium, and severe calcium deficiency is regarded as a proven cause of excessive growth of the beak.

Trimming of the beak should be left to the

Opposite: Broken feathers, which eventually loosen and are shed or removed in the course of preening, will be replaced by new feathers growing from the same site.

expert. Usually the bird puts up a good fight, and the bites of larger curved beaks can be quite painful.

Should you be faced with the unavoidable task of catching this kind of bird—your Cockatiel among them—proceed with caution.

A Cockatiel may put up a fight when being handled. Its long, curved beak can cause a good deal of pain should you be bitten by the bird.

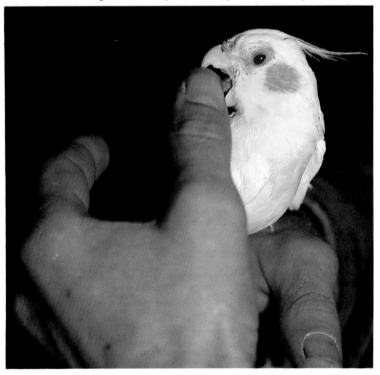

On Handling and Catching

No bird in the world likes being touched; it likes being picked up even less. Its plumage never benefits by closer contact with rough, sweaty, possibly dirty hands. The animal's fear of the much bigger human being is only increased by frequent grabbing. In the long run, however, the bird fancier cannot avoid occasionally having to keep a firm hold of or

Below: *Although the Cockatiel will not like being handled, it will eventually become necessary for the keeper to hold the bird.*

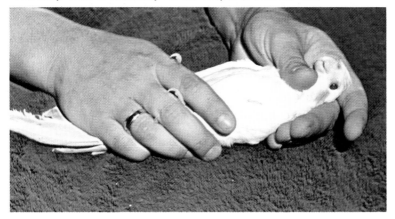

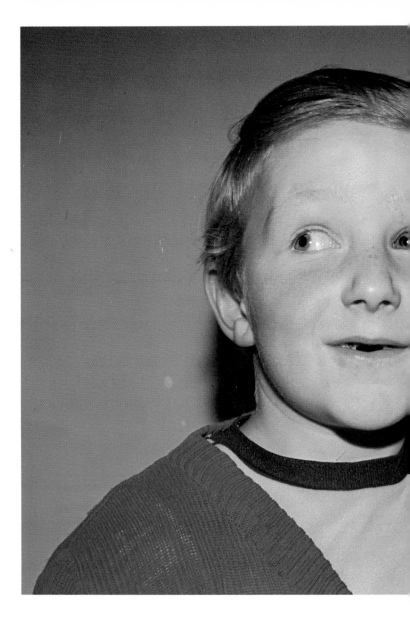

Birds can be calmed a little if talked to in a soothing manner.

catching the pet. Medicine, for instance, cannot be administered directly in any other way. The treatment of injuries and the trimming of claws and beak just mentioned would be altogether impossible otherwise.

Someone who has had no experience whatsoever dealing with his feathered friends tends to shy away from picking up a bird with the hand. And, indeed, one should never force oneself to do so! A bird

The younger a bird is, the easier it is to hand-tame it. The Cockatiel below is only four weeks old.

An older Cockatiel may take longer to tame, but it is quite possible to achieve success.

is grasped with a quick, well aimed movement from above, by which the thumb enfolds the neck and the remaining fingers, as far as possible, cover the breast and the abdomen. If the animal is turned onto its back while being taken out of the cage, its attempts to defend itself become a lot less ferocious in this unaccustomed position. The extended index finger forms a gentle vise in cooperation with the thumb. Only in this way—unless you prefer to wear leather gloves—can the sharp beak of the Cockatiel be prevented from stabbing your hand. Like most other animals in this type of situation, cage birds

Below: *Once hand-tamed, the Cockatiel is much easier to handle.*
Opposite: *By using the thumb extended as a gentle yet firm grip, you keep the Cockatiel from biting down on your hand.*

too can be calmed to a
certain extent if one
talks to them
soothingly.

During free flight all
birds show a marked
preference for perches
that are as far above
the ground as possible.
Usually this means the

curtain rod is chosen, or the lamp, or a tall cupboard, and here, safely out of reach, the bird settles down. We have already discussed that catching should never imply chasing the bird about until it grows utterly exhausted. It is better to wait until the evening, to note the animal's exact position, and to advance until the bird begins to show signs of anxiety. As soon as a kind assistant has switched off the light in the room the escapee can be caught with a single grasp, perhaps with the help of a cloth, and be put inside its familiar cage. Inside bird rooms or aviaries the use of nets is a distinct advantage. Netting requires some practice, however.

Opposite: *Cockatiels tamed when very young show little resentment toward having their feathers touched.*

The Cockatiel's Natural Talents

The Cockatiel is a bird whom nature has equipped particularly well both for running on the ground and for climbing about on trees. It thinks nothing of walking along the cage ceiling with its head suspended upside down. It loves carrying objects about in its beak. Especially marked in the Cockatiel is the talent to mimic whistling sounds. In Germany, the tune of the children's song "Hänschen klein" or of the "River Kwai March" is often used for training and in many cases with notable success.

The well feathered Cockatiel flies with endurance and great agility, escaping easily even from birds of prey. When encountering obstacles in flight it can turn back almost instantaneously.

Opposite: The Cockatiel is known for its climbing capabilities. It is an extremely agile and gymnastic bird.

Opposite: The Cockatiel is a very intelligent bird and normally understands exactly what its keeper wants from it. Right:The bird's feet, with four toes arranged in opposing pairs, are what give it its agility.

Apart from the bird's intelligent nature, it is, above all, the excellence of its gymnastic and climbing abilities that has gained it so many friends all over the world. The beak can aptly be described as the parrot's third leg. Incidentally, among the limbs of birds, it is the parrot's foot which

Due to their relatively high intelligence, Cockatiels are quite capable of being trained to perform simple acrobatic feats as well as mimicking simple whistling tunes.

what the human keeper wants from it. It has a remarkable degree of intelligence. Training it to carry out simple activities is perfectly possible. Cockatiels are very observant. If anything out of the ordinary happens, they scream loudly. Some specimens have been known in this way to give their owners fair warning of impending burglaries or of fires.

In association with humans, unless ruined by the wrong treatment during its juvenile stage, our Australian is a charming companion. I have kept nearly all the well-known pet birds from the Waxbill to the Grey Parrot and what I have just said

comes closest in similarity to the human hand.

The Cockatiel understands very well

Left and opposite: Once the Cockatiel has become familiar with its keeper and the keeper's family, it happily rests on their heads and shoulders. Cockatiels are known for being quite affectionate birds.

still holds. There is one specimen, however, I recall with something less than undiluted pleasure. It could never look at a cup on the table—full or empty— without knocking it over. Before the bird was discovered to be the culprit, the family came close to a quarrel

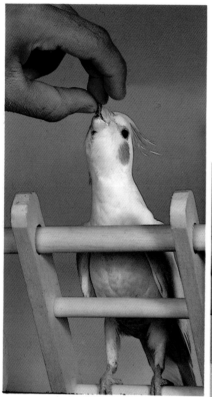

Left and below: Once they are trained and are comfortable with the keeper, Cockatiels respond to commands and will take treats and other items directly from the keeper's hands and mouth.

on several occasions. After a period of acclimatization, with close contact with the family, the Cockatiel perches contentedly on the shoulders or head of master and mistress alike and responds to commands, and anyone who talks to it is inclined to believe that the bird understands every word.

All Cockatoo species are known for their potential to become very affectionate. They lean the head against the keeper's cheek, nibble gently at his ear, and take objects or treats from his mouth. Even a tendency towards jealousy exists, as it does in certain other household pets. There are some individuals among them who clearly prefer men while others have a marked preference for women. The latter characteristic has been observed with regard to most parrot species.

Taming

The taming of any domestic pet, when all is said and done, is achieved via its stomach. That is, one gains the trust of feathered members of the household by sharing out treats. Abrupt movements or a cage site which is higher than the owner's head always have an adverse effect on taming endeavors.

How, then, is a bird which flutters about wildly inside its cage every time a member of the family approaches transformed into a devoted friend? An animal intended to attach itself to a human being, who thus has to become a substitute for the company of members of its own species, should first be made to feel really comfortable. For obvious reasons, birds which one wants to grow tame are always kept in isolation. The human being is to become their companion and

Opposite: The best and simplest way to tame your Cockatiel is to reward it with treats each time it learns something new or performs a trick previously mastered.

pastime. That there should be a period of acclimatization lasting for at least six weeks has already been discussed. During this early stage all attempts at taming are confined to frequent talking to the Cockatiel—the more frequent the better. Trying to tame a bird by depriving it of food is not a method that can be recommended. On the other hand, treats known to be special favorites can be withheld for a few days without harm to the pet and may then be

Above: *Trying to tame more than one Cockatiel at a time can be a very difficult task. This is especially true when teaching them how to speak. On most occasions the birds will pay more attention to each other than to the trainer.* ***Opposite:*** *As trust increases the bird will feel more comfortable with the owner and will become easier to train.*

offered between two fingers—at first through the bars of the cage—later through the open cage door and, as trust increases, from the hand directly in front of the perch.

If the bird takes the treat (e.g., spray millet) out of your fingers and calmly remains on its perch while doing so (it is essential that you avoid any hurried movement), you can proceed to trying to get the animal to perch on your hand. While the left hand offers the

Below: *When teaching the Cockatiel to climb onto a new perch such as a stick or your hand, continue to talk soothingly to the bird to keep it calm.* **Opposite:** *Once your bird has learned several tricks it will provide you and your company with a lot of pleasure.*

much desired treat through the bars of the cage, the index finger of the right hand—inside the cage—presses very lightly against the breast of the perching bird, about 1 cm above the thighs. Gently scratching, the finger is moved about among the pectoral feathers. Once the Cockatiel remains unafraid (after quite a few such attempts), the pressure applied by the finger can be increased sufficiently to force the bird either to climb on to the finger or to relinquish its place on the perch. Even if the Cockatiel playfully stabs at the finger in the process, never react with sudden fright. If the animal leaves the perch, follow it with the finger in slow motion and then try again. Throughout all this you should be talking in a soothing voice. The hand, complete with perching bird, should be taken out of the cage only when the small animal appears to have accepted the new perch as perfectly safe. Follow the rules that have been drawn up for free flight.

Once a cage bird is able to perch on its keeper's hand or finger without fear it is but a

Opposite: If the Cockatiel playfully nips at your hand or finger, do not panic! Don't react by quickly pulling your hand away. This will startle the bird.

small step away from the day on which it regards all members of the family as trees on whose heads, arms, and shoulders it is allowed to climb about freely. The goal of taming has been reached.

Once the Cockatiel can comfortably move on its own to your finger, it's not too far from climbing onto your head and shoulders as though they were limbs of a tree!

Learning to Talk

What learning to talk in birds ultimately comes down to is affection, which means close contact with the family is the first prerequisite. The fear of being alone soon intensifies the urge to learn, and it follows from this that it is very favorable if at least those persons which are often or always at home talk to the bird a lot, just like good mothers tend to do with their small infants.

Understandably, birds have an instinctive fear of anything that approaches them quietly or creeps up on them. No wonder, when you consider that all natural enemies stalk their prey in precisely this way! It is, however, absolutely essential that a bird one wishes to train has a feeling of security. You should therefore always approach your feathered friend from the front. In addition, the bird is a creature of habit and reacts with prolonged confusion to any change that has

Overleaf: The first step to being able to teach the bird to talk is to make it feel at ease with its keeper and his family.

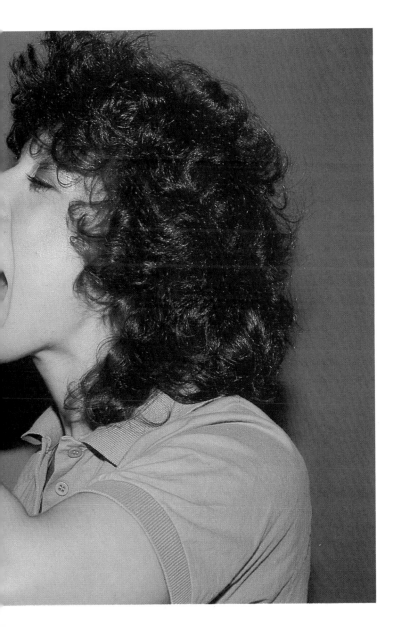

Left: The best substitute for its keeper is a training tape or record. The bird will eventually learn how to mimic the sounds made on the tape. **Opposite:** A keeper must treat his bird with kindness and love if he expects it to be willing to listen to him.

been made inside the cage or when the cage has been transferred to a different location.

The rules that must be followed when teaching a bird to talk are similar to those which apply to training a small dog. If one wants to achieve anything at all, force must never be used. What is required is a generous measure of patience, kindness and

charm (yes, towards an animal, too!), frequent practice with repetition and rewards in the case of success. A bird, easily tired after a day of unceasing play, learns most readily by the light of a standard lamp in an otherwise darkened room. Because of all the normal bird activity that is being pursued, the animals simply lack the concentration to listen during the day. The best tutor, without a doubt, is a record or a tape.

Not without good reason, the best pupils

Too many teachers tend to confuse the bird in its effort to learn, rather than accelerate the process. It takes the time and patience that few individuals have to be really successful.

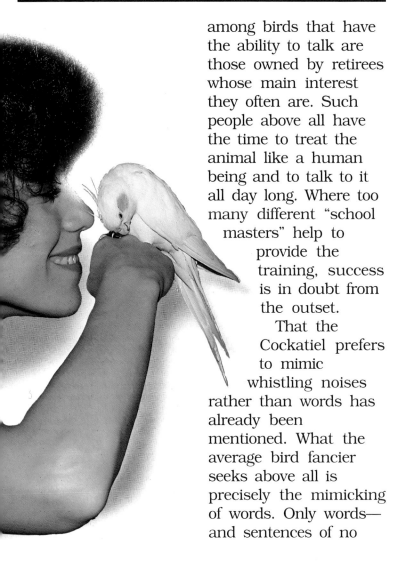

among birds that have the ability to talk are those owned by retirees whose main interest they often are. Such people above all have the time to treat the animal like a human being and to talk to it all day long. Where too many different "school masters" help to provide the training, success is in doubt from the outset.

That the Cockatiel prefers to mimic whistling noises rather than words has already been mentioned. What the average bird fancier seeks above all is precisely the mimicking of words. Only words— and sentences of no more than 5 words—repeated with great persistence, always in the same tone of voice and at the same volume, have a hope of eventually being mimicked with a greater or lesser degree of distinctiveness. A new sentence should never be attempted before the previous one has been learned and retained. Furthermore, two training sessions per day of 15 minutes each are the absolute maximum to which a Cockatiel can be subjected. It is, of course, easier to train young animals to talk or whistle than birds which are several years old.

With regard to most parrots, it has been proven that both sexes are equally talented when it comes to mimicry. Where the Cockatiel is concerned, however, the males are undeniably the more gifted sex. However, we would be asking too much even of the cock bird if we expected him to be as talented a talker as the true parrots—the Amazons, for example. Just as there are people of differing intellectual curiosity and ability, so our feathered speakers will always include a relatively large number of not-so-talented

Opposite: *Although whistling sounds are easier to learn, Cockatiels are capable of learning words and very short phrases.*

specimens. The bird to whom this book is devoted develops such a variety of other charming characteristics that one should not insist upon teaching it to mimic human sounds at any price. It is far more sensible to train it to mimic the whistling of simple tunes, which it would undoubtedly do much better.

Treatment of Minor Injuries

Incidents of this type include in-flight collision with hard objects and also getting caught on toys, wire bars, or fabrics and curtains.

A bird which has collided with a wall or a windowpane must be allowed to rest inside its cage at once and for a period of at least 24 hours. The cage should be covered. The consequences of such a collision, by the way, can still result in death

Opposite: As with other skills, talking is most readily learned by a young Cockatiel. *Below:* A proper diet is instrumental in keeping your bird strong and healthy.

days later due to migrating blood clots. It is absolutely vital for these blood clots to dissolve very gradually since there is no really effective treatment that can be given.

Among the injuries that occur relatively frequently in such a lively bird are dislocated, or at least twisted, feet with pulled tendons. Usually the keeper does not become alerted until the parakeet is seen to rest one foot and clearly avoids putting its weight on it or using it for grasping. In the majority of cases, happily, fears of anything having been fractured turn out to be groundless. The dislocations mentioned occur when the animal climbs about, perhaps with claws of excessive length, and gets caught in small toy chains or when it hangs onto a curtain during the period of free flight. It is very easy for the foot to get trapped somewhere during play inside the cage.

That a fracture has been sustained can be said with certainty only where the foot is obviously dangling loose and the bird is no longer able to move the individual toes. I cannot recommend that the reader treat leg injuries himself. Although sprains could be influenced favorably by means of infra-red ray therapy or warm camomile baths

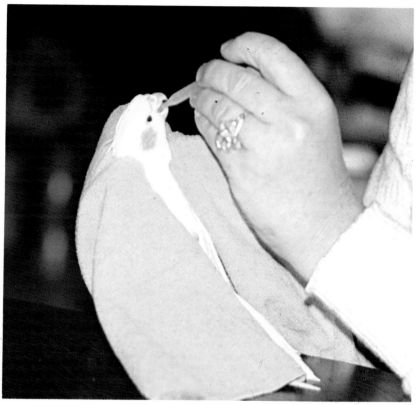

A towel is useful while holding the Cockatiel to prevent the bird from biting you. When administering medicine to the bird, a plastic eye-dropper is much better to use than a glass one. The glass eye-dropper has more of a chance of breaking and causing even more injury to your Cockatiel.

followed by massage of the limb between thumb and index finger, this is something for people who have the necessary skills. The layman just tends to cause the small animal additional pain. He should confine himself to removing all perches from the cages of birds with foot injuries, except one that has been fitted low down. The patient should not be allowed free flight again until it has made a complete recovery.

Books for bird lovers often recommend that a splint of match sticks or toothpicks

A Cockatiel chick can be injured during hand-rearing if the syringe is not handled deftly. Be careful that no food enters the bird's airway.

be applied to fractured legs with the aid of glue, cellophane tape, or nail varnish. I do not intend to repeat such nonsense here, my advice being that a bird with a fractured wing or leg be taken to the veterinary surgeon *without delay*. In this type of situation the ordinary bird fancier will find himself overtaxed when it comes to applying a

Do not try to treat injuries that are out of your league. You will probably further hurt the Cockatiel and put it through more pain.

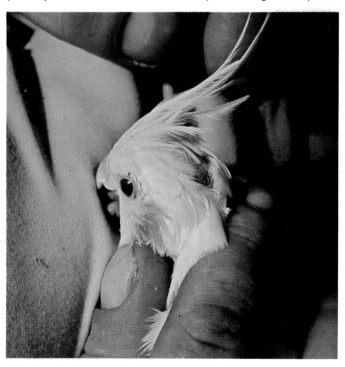

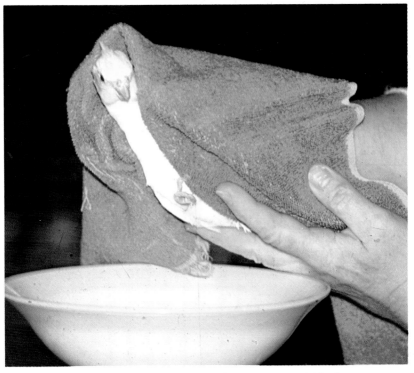

This Cockatiel is being held over steaming water to assist in the expulsion of an egg.

splint or supportive bandage to a struggling bird, however beautifully illustrated the instructions may be. He will just add to the pain the injured animal is suffering. Most petshop owners, too, if they are honest, would admit to not having the anatomical and medical knowledge necessary for this.

Legs with compound fractures often wither, like those with untreated ones, and eventually drop off of their own accord. This is not an adequate reason for having the bird put to sleep out of misguided compassion. All climbing birds adapt extraordinarily well to the absence of a limb and it soon becomes well-nigh impossible for the observer to spot their disability.

In minor injuries to the skin, special cotton-wool or a hemostyptic stick helps to arrest the bleeding. Bandages are pointless since strong birds systematically remove anything they can reach with their beaks.

Diseases

The Cockatiel is not a demanding bird where its care is concerned, nor is it prone to disease as a rule. It is a hardy, exceedingly robust and adaptable companion who can cope with more than one should expect it to. Nonetheless there is likely to come a time when your Cockatiel catches a chill. A **cold** that is being ignored can quickly turn into pneumonia. A bird with a cold generally sits about apathetically with half shut eyes and ruffled feathers. It shows none of its usual liveliness, the appetite has decreased. These signs should not go unnoticed.

The most effective remedy is a warm environment, with the temperature remaining constant. Bedside lamps (of 40–60 W) placed beside the cage have proved useful in such cases, as have infra-red heaters. An electric heating pad is suitable, too. This is

Opposite: During hand-rearing, hygiene is especially important, as illness can be transmitted from one youngster to another by the feeding implements.

put under the cage, with props between the two so that they are not in contact, and the whole arrangement is covered with a cloth on three sides and on the top.

A prerequisite for this simple method of heat therapy is that it is applied continuously—over a period of many days, if necessary—until the patient has made a complete recovery. All too often one hears that, particularly overnight, the sources of heat are switched off for reasons of safety. This is about the worst thing one could do. Just make sure that nothing can catch fire.

Labored, rhythmical breathing during which whistling noises can be heard is a clear indication of **pneumonia**. The bird's eyes are firmly shut. The body is shaking all over at brief intervals. Drafts or abrupt changes in temperature are the most common causes. Here, too, the application of heat is beneficial, but in this case it has to be combined with the administration of antibiotics. Only a vet is qualified to decide on the correct dosage or, in general, on the oral

Opposite: With most avian illnesses, the layman has difficulty distinguishing symptoms from the diseases themselves. Consultation with a veterinarian offers the best hope for efficacious treatment.

administering or injecting, of penicillin, aureomycin, streptomycin, or the often-used chlortetracyclin. The reader is most strongly advised against conducting his own experiments with the contents of the private medicine cupboard. At most, in an extreme emergency, small fragments of an aspirin can be added to the drinking water. It is now appropriate to supply water that has been boiled. The author has made successful attempts to treat diseases of the respiratory system by putting affected birds into the smallest cages possible inside a cardboard box the walls

Part of a Cockatiel's alimentary tract, which shows a posterior section of the duodenum impacted with a large group of roundworms.

of which had been internally covered with a menthol-camphor ointment (available without a prescription).

Scaly face, i.e., horn-like proliferations of a crumbly nature at the sides of the beak and around the eyes, is neither transmissible to human beings nor

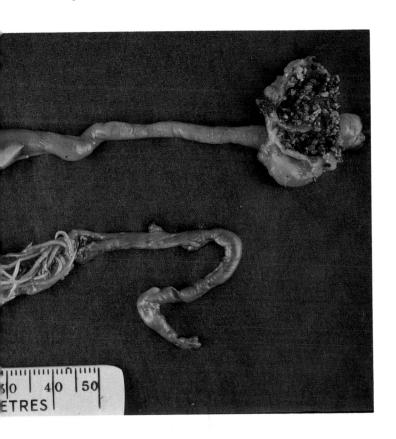

endangering the animal's life. Unfortunately this phenomenon is rapidly transmitted to members of the same species and to Budgerigars. The causal agents are mange mites. Treatment with Odylen, painted onto the affected areas, is recommended. This drug must be administered very carefully to avoid getting any **in** the eyes.

Every bird suffers from **diarrhea** a few times during its lifespan. It is caused by excess, wet, or rotten greenstuff, the chewing of wallpaper or house plants, by food which is

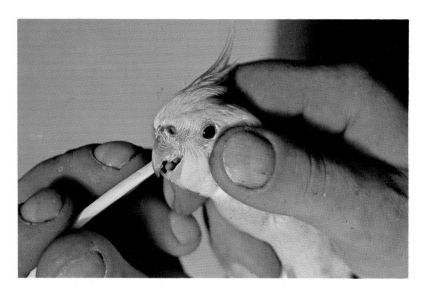

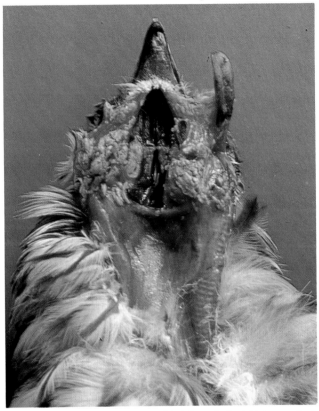

Above: *The buccal cavity of a bird that died of trichomoniasis. The deposits become so attached that any attempts at removal would cause serious hemorrhaging. Death from this type of infection normally results from the inability to swallow food.* **Opposite:** *Although careful visual examination is the first step in combating illness, keep in mind that this will be stressful for even the tamest Cockatiel.*

too old and, above all, food that has grown dusty. Anyone who allows his Cockatiel to partake of roast meat, butter, cheese, or alcoholic beverages should not be surprised about subsequent digestive upsets.

Diarrhea would not give such cause for concern; if untreated, it might not develop into intestinal inflammation. For this reason, every responsible animal keeper checks up on the bird's feces at regular intervals. In the case of very liquid diarrhea, fruit and green food should be withheld at once and the cage must be cleaned every day. Instead of drinking water, unsweetened black tea or peppermint tea are recommended. A cure is effected more speedily if anti-diarrheal drugs for birds are given as well.

Severe diarrhea results in complete debility. Once the feces contain traces of blood, all help may be coming too late. In serious cases like that, consult the veterinary surgeon! The application of heat of up to 30°C invariably boosts the effect of drugs. A prophylactic agent should always be at hand. Mild diarrhea is hardly likely to develop into a fatal intestinal infection if the keeper notices it and treats it in time.

Diseases of the liver, which for many

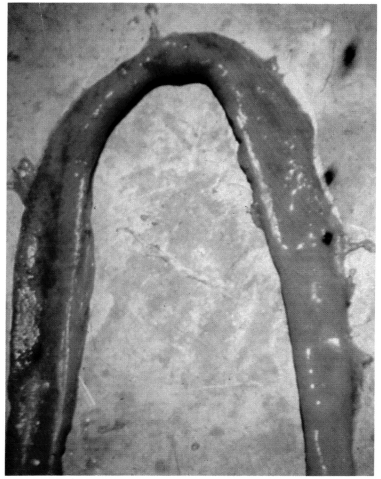

In this bird, Coccidiosis has caused petechial hemorrhages of the intestinal mucosa.

different reasons are on the increase among stocks of ornamental birds and probably often have their origin in the wrong food or in feeding mistakes, fortunately are less common in the robust Cockatiel. An early diagnosis and a cure are virtually impossible. That a hepatic disease was present almost invariably comes to light only during the examination by an expert of ornamental birds that have died.

Consumption occurs particularly in Cockatiels which are forced to vegetate in unsuitable surroundings. Notably, birds in damp, cold rooms, basements, and sheds are susceptible to this form of avian tuberculosis, which is

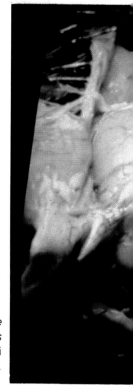

The small lesions of white focal areas in the liver, congested pectoral muscles, pericarditis and peritonitis are all signs of E. coli *septicemia.*

otherwise rare and is not transmitted to humans. Degenerate strains are predisposed to it. In the case of rapid, abnormal weight loss, seek veterinary advice and take fresh fecal specimens along with you for examination. These make the correct diagnosis much easier.

Psittacosis, today

more aptly termed **ornithosis** (bird disease) since almost 130 different species of birds are now known at least to be carriers of it, has lost much of its past terror since the effective antibiotics were discovered. The keeper of an individual bird which has recovered from the disease has little cause for concern as a subsequent infection is extremely rare.

The government of the German Federal Republic has long since put an end to the practice of having stocks of birds infected with ornithosis compulsorily destroyed. After international experiments with vaccinations proved

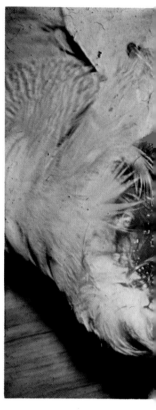

unsuccessful, the destruction practiced in the past has been replaced by the antibiotic chlortetracyclin, which

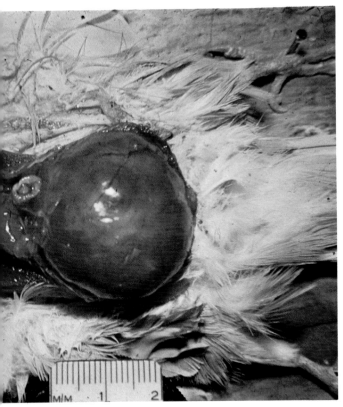

In this bird the heart has been displaced because the cystic neoplasm of the kidney takes up so much of the abdominal cavity.

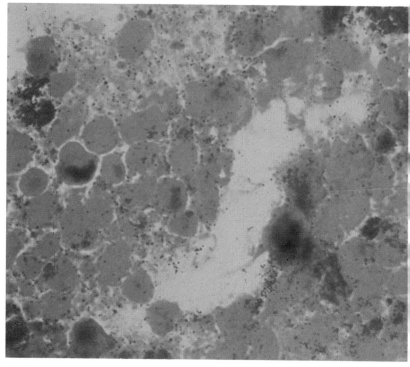

This microscope slide has been stained and magnified 1000 times in order to show the Chlamyidae in the air sac of a psittacine bird with psittacosis.

achieved excellent results with regard to killing a causal agent which represents an intermediate stage between a virus and a bacterium and is so tiny that it can be spread through dust. Where the disease is suspected one of two methods of treatment can be chosen with the aid of the veterinary surgeon: Intra-muscular injection (an injection into the muscle) of a comparatively high dose or the oral (by mouth) administration of a food to which chlortetracyclin has been added. The latter has to be carried out for a minimum of 21 days, extended a total of 45 days where the presence of the disease has been established. Once the result of the official examination has confirmed the infection, the bird fancier no longer has a choice. From now on the veterinary surgeon is in authority and, along with giving other instructions, is likely to prescribe a special medicated complete food which is to form the sole source of nourishment. The periods of treatment have been laid down. Whether treatment has been successful is determined by an examination after its completion.

Consideration for his family's health, his own health and that of his fellow creatures should urge every breeder to have the examination performed if there is any reason to suspect an incident of the disease, and to budget for the necessary treatment if the result of the analysis is positive. The cost of treatment is minimal as compared with the value of the birds, the majority of which will be saved by it.

A less pleasant side effect of the administration of antibiotics via the digestive tract, both in man and in animals, is the partial destruction of the intestinal flora, i.e., of a group of bacteria which need to be present inside the intestine to effect digestion. I would strongly advise aviculturists who have not had to deal with this problem before to discuss with their veterinary surgeon how the addition of vitamins to the drinking water might prevent intestinal upsets. Vitamins of the B-complex are particularly valuable.

The problem of psittacosis/ornithosis and its control is not likely to become less pressing in the

foreseeable future since this disease can also be spread by birds which, although clinically healthy, are hosts and carriers of the causal agents. Nor is it possible, in the light of present scientific knowledge, to achieve permanent immunization by means of therapy with antibiotics. Various ideas about medical treatment have a habit of instilling unnecessary fear in the reading public. We must not play these matters down. On the other hand, it is good to bear the following in mind. The risk to man from birds has so far been no greater than that

This photo shows the development of airsacculitis in the abdominal air sac due to psittacosis.

of contracting other zoonoses, i.e., diseases of animals transmissible to humans (including rabies, for instance). The statistics prove that the disease rarely runs a fatal course in human beings. Over the last 35 years thousands of parrots have passed through the author's hands and yet he has never once contracted ornithosis, any more than have the many fellow aviculturists he is acquainted with. You are advised, therefore, to trust in your luck and, above all, not to waste any money on those dubious prophylactic agents that sometimes appear on the market. Even more dangerous are experiments with antibiotics that have been obtained without a prescription. You are urged, in your own best interest, to refrain from such experiments. The administration via the drinking water never achieves the only effective blood level of at least 1 mcg/ml that has to be maintained for a prescribed period. All one accomplishes, if a drug which is normally effective against a disease is given at too low a

Opposite: Since Cockatiels hull seeds, eating only the kernel, administration of medicines and nutritional supplements in the diet is usually not practical.

dosage, is that the causal agents become resistant to the drug. This has the undesirable consequence that, in the event of a genuine outbreak of the infection the drug concerned remains ineffective—a widely feared medical problem of the present age.

A Cockatiel that is being well looked after in its separate cage or small numbers of birds in a hobbyist's aviary of the correct construction are seldom threatened by disease. A lifespan of 15 to 20 healthy years is nothing unusual. The **molt** (casting of feathers) is not a sign of disease but a necessary process of regeneration for all birds. Of course the keeper can make this period of increased demands on the metabolism easier by providing a varied diet and plenty of dietary supplements with a high vitamin content. Spraying with tepid water, as mentioned earlier, is of particular

Offering a Cockatiel a bath will help it to keep its plumage in the best of condition.

benefit to the bird during this time. Chemical agents, on the other hand, are of little practical value. When parts of the plumage are lost outside the normal molting periods, one can deduce either that the bird has caught a chill as a result of drafts or a drop in temperature, that it has suffered some unusual fright, or that it has been receiving the wrong food. The bad habit of allowing birds to have food meant for human consumption is often the cause of chronic molt.

Less pleasant, since there is no real remedy for it, is **feather-plucking**, a phenomenon which has been known and feared for decades, especially with regard to parrot-like birds. At one time it was attributed to the boredom experienced by animals kept in isolation, but it is very much more likely that the birds chew feather quills in an attempt to make up for nutritional deficiencies. It is still more unpleasant when breeding pairs pluck each other, or even their offspring, to the point of baldness. And it would happen that the tendency is to start with the greatest asset of this species—the crest! This habit was already mentioned in books written at the turn of the century, but to date the science of ornithology has not been able to come up with a genuine cure. Experts recommend that twigs from fruit trees be given at regular intervals all the year 'round, these containing valuable nutrients particularly when the buds are forming. (Beware of trees that have been sprayed!). The bark on these twigs is completely peeled off by the parakeets, which also ensures a certain amount of distraction from feather-plucking. Lime, in the form described earlier, should be provided throughout the year, notably during the

Opposite: To help prevent against feather-plucking, experts suggest that a keeper place fruit tree twigs in his bird's diet on a regular basis.

molting period.

Of a corrective, rather than therapeutic, value is a derivative of the antibiotic known as chloramphenicol.

Normally effective against fungal diseases and eczema, it has a lasting bitter taste without being toxic. It is, therefore, well suited for the behavior modification of notorious pluckers. The healing of wounds is speeded up.

If you are interested in trying this course of treatment, you should consult your veterinarian.

Perching on one leg is no cause for concern. Only weakened or very young birds rest on both legs because they are not yet able to balance on one. The leg which is temporarily retracted into the abdominal plumage has the weight taken off it and is being warmed, and that is the reason for such a posture.

Only exceptionally will a Cockatiel fail to distinguish between gnawing on a toy and eating food.

Needless to say, the bird fancier should examine and attend to the feet of his charges at regular intervals. Feet covered in excreta, often just a sign of insufficient cleanliness, may of course point towards intestinal upsets, since healthy droppings are not smeary. Clean the feet by washing them with tepid water, and check up on the cloacal region, which will also be dirty if the bird is suffering from digestive trouble. Occasional doses of charcoal for animal use will help

prevent dangerous attacks of diarrhea.

Mange mites reveal their presence by forming scab-like deposits on the feet and thighs. Appropriate drugs, which are painted onto the affected areas, are available at the petshop. Injuries to the claws generally heal up quickly without requiring treatment, even if they bleed copiously at first. Hemostyptic cotton wool can be used on the injuries.

In older Cockatiels the legs grow rough and this can lead to the ring becoming embedded. It is better to remove the ring in good time with a small pair of sharp scissors which are moved along the inside of the leg. Once the leg has become inflamed or severely swollen, i.e., the ring has grown into it and is cutting off the blood supply, amputation is often necessary.

It is not necessary, notably with regard to the robust Cockatiel, to deal in detail with other, more uncommon signs of disease. While the owner of an individual bird would always do well to seek veterinary advice when there is something wrong with his pet, the aviculturist can, for comparatively little money, obtain the information necessary for treating sick birds himself.

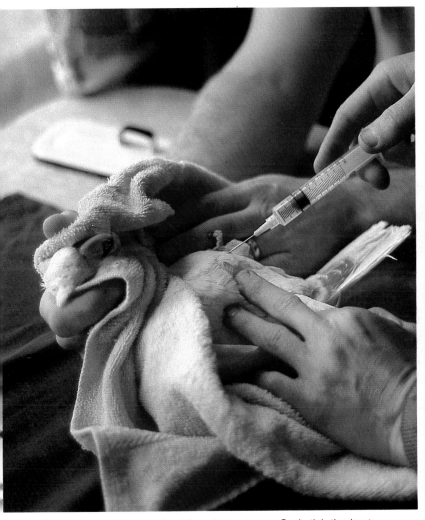

If you are ever unsure about how to treat your Cockatiel, the best thing to do is to consult your veterinarian.

Mites are parasites that cannot be completely guarded against. Even birds in the cleanest cages are capable of getting mites.

Parasites

Like all birds, whether living free or inside a cage, the Cockatiel can become infested with mites. The danger of this happening is greater in the summer than in the winter. Petshop owners have noticed that bird fanciers tend to be ashamed of this matter and seldom have the courage to purchase a remedy for mites without protesting at great length how particular they are in regard to cleanliness. It is high time, then, for it to be stated explicitly that an infestation with mites in cage birds does not imply a lack of cleanliness on the keeper's part; it is something that really cannot be prevented entirely. Mites, and their eggs in particular, get inside houses through the tiniest cracks with the dust. Pigeons and sparrows, as well as the so-called woodland birds, usually have mites and ensure their distribution.

If your pet has got these troublesome pests, the minute arachnids will barely be recognizable with the unaided eye. Hiding inside cracks in the cage or a few meters away inside gaps in the furniture or the wallpaper and molding during the day, they come streaming out after dark and suck the bird's blood like mosquitos. They multiply rapidly by means of eggs from which new mites hatch after a short period. Most chemical agents kill only the insects and not the eggs that have been laid. Since the bird is reached via the perch, good results at

A group of feather lice on the underside of the wing.

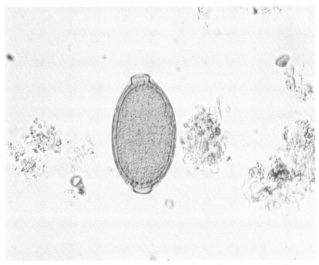

A threadworm egg as seen through the microscope during examination of feces.

control can be achieved by rubbing special insecticides into this. Mite powder is sprinkled into all the corners and cracks. The cage and its surroundings are quickly dealt with by means of aerosols.

The reader will note that treatment of the bird has not been mentioned at all. For a very good reason! The manufacturers generally stress that their insecticides are not harmful to the birds. This is perfectly correct, provided the small animals do not end up being absolutely covered in powder, or get sprayed from close range so that they become dripping wet. The author has seen hundreds of birds die in agony due to chemical treatment.

It should not be too difficult to grasp that chemical agents capable of killing insects just through contact must, by definition, be *poisonous*. One exception is formed by those insecticides which block the tiny respiratory passages of the parasites, thus causing death by asphyxia. Contact insecticides, although only mildly toxic to larger animals, do have a noticeable, and at times dangerous, effect if applied in greater amounts. Therefore the parasites can be adequately controlled by treating the cages without their inmates, provided the surrounding area and the cage site are also treated. Despite relevant reassurances by the manufacturers in their enclosed leaflets, food and drinking water should be removed before treatment since a good

Opposite: A magnified view of a typical biting louse, which can be found in the feathers of a bird.

Take precautions to keep the Cockatiel away from too much contact with insecticides no matter how "harmless" they are supposed to be to the bird. Parasites can be properly controlled by treating the cage and surrounding areas.

dose of chemicals will do nothing to improve them, however harmless the insecticides may supposedly be. Measures for the control of parasites are most effective early in the morning or towards the evening. Treating the birds themselves would not make a lot of sense in any case since their bodies seldom harbor any mites in the daytime.

A New Generation in One's Own Home

Sooner or later every genuine bird lover would like his pets to reproduce. Breeding Cockatiels is comparatively easy, which means the wish can come true if one buys or hires a bird of the opposite sex. Since it is always advisable to abide by the law, I need to point out that in some countries a license is required for breeding parrots and parakeets (even if only one pair is involved!). It is irrelevant in this respect whether the progeny are to be kept,

When beginning a breeding program, always start with the best stock possible.

given away, or sold.

If we talk about young birds in the home, we obviously want to avoid any extensive preparations if we possibly can. Already available is the cage, which is of adequate size. What we need to buy in addition is the nest-box which will serve as cradle. Likewise the partner, of course, if not already acquired.

Breeding has the best chance of success if the animals are used to free flight in the home and spend more time outside their cage. In this case the nest-box

Cockatiels, like other parrots, lay white eggs. Several days after hatching, the sheaths encasing the feathers emerge from the chick's skin.

It would be unwise to remove the cock from the cage too early. Both male and female birds take turns sitting on the egg and feeding the chicks.

is hung up on the wall (make sure it is secure) or put on top of a cupboard, or on a windowsill, from where it need never be moved. A perching-rod fixed high up on the wall for the birds to fly onto is strongly recommended. One may be lucky and find that the birds start breeding the very first time a nest-box is attached to the cage. This seldom happens, however.

Since there is in any case virtually nothing the aviculturist can do to promote mating, egg-laying, and incubating, his task is purely one of patient waiting and of preventing all disturbances. It is important, also, to ensure that the light inside the room is not thoughtlessly switched off in the evenings if the brooding hen happens to be outside her nest-box at that moment. A weak night light of 15 watts is an advantage.

The incubation period extends over 19 to 21 days—since one can never be absolutely certain when the birds started sitting. The Cockatiels are model parents and take turns to sit on the eggs and, later, to feed the chicks. It would thus be misguided to remove the cock.

Notice the wing development of a chick only nine days old.

Buying Breeding Birds

It is by no means more difficult to let an optically pleasing and, above all, normal and healthy new generation grow up in captivity than it is, by selecting the wrong parent animals, providing poor accommodation or inadequate care, to raise stunted or deformed young birds. Since the modern bird fancier is cost-conscious and sometimes finances his

Opposite: Keepers interested in breeding attractive chicks take great care finding the proper parents for their needs. *Above:* This pair of Cockatiels is mating near a tree trunk, which serves as their nest.

beautiful hobby in part by selling the young birds he has bred, this alone would turn the production of unattractive Cockatiels into a waste of time and money.

If one takes a serious interest in breeding Cockatiels, the correct purchase of breeding pairs is of the greatest importance. In fact, it may be the most important prerequisite of all! The comparative eagerness of the Cockatiel to reproduce itself has come to mean

Above: *The combination of the Lutino and Pearl mutations produces attractive youngsters that will delight any Cockatiel breeder.*
Opposite: *Both members of the breeding pair should be good specimens if the breeder wishes to produce chicks of similar quality.*

that due to successive breeding over a prolonged period, without the introduction of new blood, one gets strains which are inferior. This poor quality reveals itself in shabby plumage, a curved back, dwarfism, chronic molt, crippled feet, and a permanent inability to fly. Birds which the observer finds unappealing at first sight will seldom produce attractive descendants. Breeding birds should be fully grown and show the full adult coloration, as well as being of normal size, pleasing to look at, alert and lively.

It is expedient not to allow Cockatiels to breed until they have fully completed their first year, although sexual maturity is already attained at eight to nine months. Where there is a difference in age between the breeding pair offered, it should preferably be the hen who is the younger partner.

The longer one is able to quietly and unhurriedly observe the birds one is thinking of buying the better, and the less anyone presses for a decision the better. It is not a bad idea to turn to an aviculturist who has a special preference for these birds and is able to offer an opinion. A conversation with someone like that is always interesting and

A mated pair will typically sit close together much like this gray male and pearl female.

Although one can take steps to improve the chances of a good pair and successful breeding, there is always a certain amount of luck involved as well.

profitable. A slightly higher price would seem a good investment, all the more so if a guarantee of descent and suitability for breeding is obtained. To ensure the birds are of different blood, the purchaser should try to avoid acquiring birds which are closely related, although in practice this is often not possible because the prospective buyer is either unaware of it or not given the information.

It would be wrong, in this book of advice, to condemn the purchase of breeding birds from petshops. Many beginners who live in cities simply do not see any alternative. It is possible to get a very good deal indeed, but might I point out objectively that in shops the buyer often receives nest-siblings since petshop owners buy up the whole brood. It should be equally indisputable that aviculturists offer to private persons the best birds they have raised in captivity. Even the novice can, after a good, long look, avoid buying birds of the same sex where these are being offered as a "breeding-pair."

Finally, a bit of luck also comes into the selection. No one can be certain, after all, that the would-be partners are going to get on and will in fact proceed to mate. Some birds are infertile, which unfortunately is something one cannot tell just by looking at them.

Professional Breeding

In addition to age and selection, proper housing is a key element of a good breeding plan.

It may be hard to believe, but a Cockatiel originating from the tropical zones can cope with our climate out-of-doors regardless of the season—which includes winters with lots of snow and temperatures below freezing point—if the bird is given the proper type of housing. There simply is no more natural way of keeping the majority of birds than to accommodate them in an outdoor enclosure with light, air, and sun. Because of air pollution, industrial areas are excepted, of course. Birds kept in aviaries in such areas are unsightly even if roofing has been put up.

Like the Budgerigars, which have also come to us from Australia, Cockatiels nest inside hollow trees or in

Opposite: Allowing birds to choose their own mating partners creates better results than just putting two Cockatiels together.

cavities. They gnaw into soft wood. They also breed when kept in association with other species of birds, which, although sometimes leading to minor squabbles, actually increases the desire to breed. Letting the birds select their own partners is better than using any kind of persuasion.

There should be a choice of at least two nest boxes per breeding pair. The minimum in aviaries would be three nesting facilities for every two breeding pairs.

Cockatiels, like some other kinds of birds, cannot be "forced" into a breeding unit of the keeper's choosing.

Ideal for breeding Cockatiels is an enclosure which, after the breeding partners have chosen one another and the birds have selected a nesting facility, can be partitioned off (with the partitions on stand-by until required) to ensure that each pair has its own territory. Alternatively, separate compartments for each pair should be provided. Visual contact is not harmful. An addition of several pairs of Budgerigars to the aviary ensures that the latter is more fully utilized.

The nutritional requirements of the adult birds during the breeding period are exactly the same as at any other time. Special

Once a pair of Cockatiels have selected each other for mating, they should be placed in a separate compartment to ensure that each pair has its own territory.

arrangements on the breeder's part in that respect are, therefore, superfluous. The clutch can consist of anything from three to eight eggs, which are laid on alternate mornings and, when the clutch is complete, are incubated by the hen for a period of 20 days. To enable her to feed herself, the cock often takes over for the hen. Alternatively, she stays inside the nest box and is fed by her partner. As compared with large parakeets, the large number of eggs produced by the Cockatiels per clutch must be described as unique.

The habit often observed in wild birds, in which the cock tends to sit on the eggs during the day while the hen prefers to incubate over night, also applies to the vast majority of domesticated Cockatiels.

It would thus be a serious mistake to remove the cock as soon as the hen has started to sit on the eggs, however often one may do this with regard to other bird species during the incubation period. It is essential to examine the nest boxes at regular intervals of three days at the most. These check ups would seem particularly appropriate where one has not seen one or the other of the adult birds for some time. Chicks or young birds that have died are also spotted in this way, and before any unpleasant odor draws one's attention to them. The chicks should, if possible, always be carried out at a time when both birds have left the immediate

Having left the nest, a young Cockatiel will sample the foods available, guided by what its parents choose to eat.

vicinity of the nest box. Characteristic is the hissing noise made by incubating hens, and indeed by juvenile birds, when one approaches the nest.

That the chicks have hatched successfully becomes apparent from the relatively loud begging noises. Now both parents untiringly feed the hungry brood.

For the feeding of the rapidly growing nestlings some hobbyists supplement the usual diet of seeds with hard boiled egg (mashed) and mixed with rusk-flour, white bread soaked in milk, a commercial raising food, or similar— usually soft—additions which may also include germinated seeds. It is suggested that the reader ask a fellow breeder to show him how to prepare germinated food, as this can be valuable all the year 'round.

Although the animals usually accept these supplements very readily, it must be borne in mind that any soft food quickly ferments in the summer and then becomes a killer where the brood is concerned. On the other hand, foods served straight from the refrigerator to delay fermentation have also been known to kill young parakeets because they were too cold for them. Spray millet in bigger quantities is always harmless.

Prior to the onset of breeding, the Cockatiel parents should be accustomed to a diet on which they will be able to rear their chicks successfully.

Rearing to independence proceeds quite without assistance from the breeder. No wonder, then, that breeding Cockatiels is said to be easy! The young birds leave the box about four and a half weeks after hatching but are then fed for at least another 14 days on the perch outside.

Sexing is easy where adult birds are concerned but not so simple when it comes to juveniles whose external appearance is similar to that of the hens. While one can hope to be able to sex birds from spring broods by the fall, young birds produced in the fall are considerably more difficult to categorize. The reason for this is that in the latter the juvenile molt begins later, often in fact as late as in the coming spring.

Some keepers complain that they do not know at what point they should separate the young from their parents. Certainly there is a danger, if this is left too late, that it may be more difficult to distinguish the juveniles from the breeding hen. But a closer look will reveal some differences that can still be seen to exist. This is said in case one wants to avoid checking the ring numbers.

Separating the young birds from their parents

would only become a matter of urgency if squabbles were to break out. Among birds of their size, Cockatiels are, however, justly regarded as particularly peaceable and as a rule do not make use of their superior physical

With Cockatiels kept outdoors, seasonal changes may affect the tempo of the youngsters' development and molting.

strength even to intimidate the smallest of Waxbills.

If among your juvenile birds you observe individuals which are constantly losing feathers and growing new ones which themselves are shed before they are fully developed, then there is good reason to suspect these birds of being "runners," i.e., of suffering from the disease known as French molt. This is a developmental disturbance and, as has been proven, not a phenomenon connected with domestication. The search for the cause has been occupying ornithologists for over half a century, so far without success. Some experts believe that mites are present which destroy the still very soft quills of the newly sprouted feathers. A diet with little variation and insufficient protein during the raising period appears to aid the disease. Breeding pairs that have produced young animals with this tendency must on no account be used for breeding again. Much has since come to light which would indicate that French molt can be traced back to the concurrence of certain hereditary factors. Animals, just like human beings, can, however, be carriers of hereditary factors that did not become manifest in themselves

French molt, a disorder where a bird continually loses feathers before they have completely developed, is now thought to be a result of hereditary factors. The two parents of such birds shouldn't be used.

but only become dominant in the next generation or the one after. A matching that, when living conditions are good, results in "runners" among the progeny is unsuitable, even if the two partners themselves appear to be in excellent condition.

A Lutino Cockatiel exhibiting the characteristic white body with yellow and orange-red in its plumage.

Mutations and Their Inheritance

Unlike the Budgerigar, the Cockatiel, now also regarded as domesticated, held back for a long time before presenting us with mutations. Around 1950 some pied variations occurred in the U.S.A. for the first time ever and initially were systematically developed further in that country. Consequently, the first pairs did not reach Europe until ten years later and, not surprisingly, were very expensive to buy. That notwithstanding, their culture has made very good progress in all European countries since then, for, happily, these pied Cockatiels did not by any means turn out to be a deleterious mutation but, rather, proved to be particularly easy to raise, prolific, and hardy. Hence the price of such a pair has dropped to a level that is within most people's means.

The so-called white or, more accurately, Lutino Cockatiels are not in fact pure white. Rather, the yellow as well as the orange-red colors in their plumage have been preserved, which makes these birds absolutely enchanting to look at. With their bright-yellow head, its crest of the same color, and the more striking orange-red patches on the cheeks, they remind one of miniature Cockatoos, far more even than the wild-colored Cockatiels—

Predominantly clear pieds like this one can be very appealing to the eye.

except that they are still more alluring and graceful and have more richly contrasting colors at the same time. In adult birds the whole plumage has a pale yellow hue while the hen's tail is of a more intense yellow, rather like that of the wild bird. Another asset of these Cockatiels is the fact that the females are virtually as beautiful in color as the males who show less yellow. In adult birds the latter's tail is of a purer white, too. Here a characteristic crops up again that was not mentioned at the beginning of the book when the wild-colored bird was described: namely, that the tail of the adult cock is uniformly slate-gray whereas that of the hen has yellow transverse bands. Because some pigment (psittacin) has been preserved, one cannot talk about an Albino Cockatiel. Rather, it should be called a "Lutino," which means nothing more than albino plus pigment (lutein = yellow coloring matter). Since the different strains of "clear" Cockatiels in Germany vary in the extent and intensity of yellow, some breeders offer "Albinos," others "Lutinos," which is somewhat misleading as golden-yellow Lutinos cannot exist, whatever some advertisements say to the contrary. Both forms have dark red eyes however, i.e., there is no dark pigment in the eye, with the result that the blood shows through. That is always a sign of true albinism. In addition, there are now also black-eyed yellow and white Cockatiels of partially dominant inheritance. These are becoming increasingly important.

The inheritance of albinotic Cockatiels is sex-linked, the briefest explanation, in practical terms, of this being that only the cock can directly pass on this color direct. When a white cock is mated to a wild-colored female, only white to yellow daughters and gray sons result, all of whom are themselves heterozygous.

Conversely, a red-eyed female paired with a gray (wild-colored) cock produces only gray young of both sexes, but once again all the sons are heterozygous. A heterozygous cock with a lutino hen yields 50% lutino young of both sexes and 50% gray of whom all the cocks are again heterozygous. This pairing is practiced by many aviculturists who attach great importance to receiving robust young of both colors and sexes whereby they can, at the same time, guarantee that the gray cocks in lutino are heterozygotes. A pair of pure lutinos produces a progeny which, in turn, is exclusively lutino. This is another pairing

The dark red color in this Cockatiel's eyes is a sign of true albinism.

which is now often practiced. As long as the pairs are well cared for and not exploited (no more than three broods in one year; thereafter the nest boxes must be removed), that is perfectly acceptable. It is only thanks to this rapid increase in numbers that prices have dropped to a normal level. Pure albinotic pairs also produce a vigorous and healthy progeny, provided there has been no inbreeding. On the contrary, white and yellow Cockatiels are often bigger and stronger than wild-colored ones, as well as presenting with prettier and fuller crests. Only on the back of the head do Cockatiels from lutino x lutino often have a patch where the plumage is very thin. If this gets out of hand, crossing with wild-colored birds becomes necessary. The pairing of heterozygous cock x wild-colored hen is inadvisable. While this, too, yields an instant 25% of lutino hens, one only gets 50% of heterozygous cocks that look exactly like the rest and can be identified only through test pairing in the next generation.

At the time of writing, a good pairing for the breeding of Cockatiels straight from the nest is: Lutino cock x wild-colored hen. This results in red-eyed females and wild-

Notice the beautiful colors on the wings and tail of this Golden Pearl Cockatiel.

colored cocks only, which means when the young are ready for taming at six to eight weeks their sex can already be guaranteed. Normally the latter is not possible with absolute certainty where Cockatiels are concerned until they are about five months old.

The "clear" Cockatiel with its yellow crest and red cheeks is ideally suited to become "the poor man's Cockatoo." When I say "poor" I do not necessarily mean financially restricted

A pair of Pearl Cockatiel adults with the typical orange-red spots on the cheek.

but, rather, limited as far as space is concerned. In other words: in a modern city flat this miniature Cockatoo is more easily accommodated as a welcome household pet than, for instance, the Lesser Sulphur-Crested Cockatoo which, although here quoted as a comparably small species, is still considerably larger. Over and above that, just as with the true Cockatoos, the bird's sex is of no consequence where attractiveness and amiability are concerned, unless of course there is a strong preference for a cock because of its greater talent for mimicking.

As already mentioned, the markings of the pied Cockatiels—in gray, yellow, and white—can also be very appealing. The most handsome among them—and this applies to both sexes—have very full crests of a pure yellow color while the rest of the plumage is more or less irregularly spotted. With regard to most pied races, however, heredity does not seem to fall into any particular pattern on which the breeder might base his selection. Rather, the attraction of breeding pieds lies in the constant surprises it brings since virtually no two birds ever look exactly alike. The attraction for the private hobbyist who wants a single bird is that he can choose a pied bird to suit his individual taste, i.e., a lighter or a darker animal.

Inheritance is partially dominant insofar as a pied bird, irrespective of sex, paired with a pure wild-colored partner, already produces so-called "head-spot pieds" in the first generation. These are chiefly wild-colored Cockatiels with a few light spots of varying size on the head and neck, or they may have a few light-colored flight or tail feathers, and in some cases both these characteristics are present. Such pieds mated among each other or, better still, paired with a pied partner with more light color than themselves then produce still "clearer" pieds with beautiful markings. By breeding from two predominantly light-colored pieds it has since been possible, purely by means of selection, to produce the equally popular yellow and white Cockatiels with black eyes.

In other respects there is no connection between pieds and lutinos. They are two different mutations; if, for example, one mates a pied cock to a lutino female, the result will be mainly wild-colored young which have only those light spots on the head again and among which the cocks are heterozygous for lutino. In other words, they do not influence each other genetically.

Pearled and Marginated Cockatiels were produced, by selective breeding, in the German Federal Republic from 1967 onwards and not much later they also occurred in the U.S.A. At first they sold at fantastic prices; they are now on the market in adequate numbers at normal prices. Their unusual markings have gained them many friends. Both sexes have bright red patches on the cheeks and dark crests. Their wings are dark, with light transverse bands in the lower third. When the wing is folded, this has the effect of producing what is described as a "mirror." The tail feathers are yellow, with dark shafts. The Pearled Cockatiels have yellowish to whitish speckles above, which includes the coverts. In

The term Lutino *comes from the word* lutein, *which is the yellow coloring matter that appears in the crest of these mutations.*

the Marginated Cockatiels the speckles are more on the dark side, with light borders, which makes the markings look even more richly contrasting. In a slightly blurred form, the pearled or marginated pattern continues on the chest, and on the rump it results in narrow bands. The dark basic coloration varies from gray to black.

The inheritance of both forms is sex linked, and they are alleles (i.e., very closely related). Aviculturists differentiate between Golden and Silver Pearled or Marginated, depending on whether the color of the markings is more yellow or more white.

Birds with golden markings are the most sought after. Pearled and Marginated Cockatiels already show this contrastive pattern when they leave the nest box and are sometimes at their most beautiful in the juvenile plumage. For commercial reasons, the fact that the markings of old cocks virtually disappear and are replaced by wild-colored, dark gray feathers was withheld for a long time. Some birds show just a few pearled feathers on the top late in life. In some hens the pearling also diminishes when they grow old, although not to the same extent. Both sexes, however, continue to pass the pattern on intact and their young once again emerge from the nest box with the same beautiful markings. For this reason, only Pearled or Marginated Cockatiels of the female sex are shown at exhibitions.

Due to continued mixing of Pearled and Marginated, we often find that both patterns are present on one and the same bird. It would, therefore, be better to speak of "Marked" Cockatiels.

Because of the color change in the cocks, some aviculturists now prefer to breed Marked Cockatiels in

This Pied Pearled Cockatiel has characteristic white spots. Notice the yellow on the white feathers.

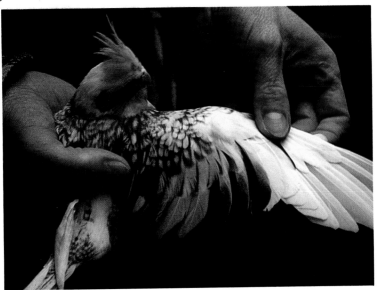

combination with Pieds, which is made comparatively easy by their dominant inheritance. Pearled and Marginated Cockatiels then show pearling or margination on the dark upper parts of the plumage. In combination with the lighter areas, which are either yellow or white, this results in extremely colorful Cockatiels which, apart from the pearling in the cocks, remain so even when they are old. All of them have intense reddish-brown patches on the cheeks and the majority have bright yellow crests and tails.

In Cinnamon Cockatiels the black pigment is absent from the wild-colored plumage. This mutation can also be seen in many birds of other species—and, indeed, many species of other animals—that have become domesticated. What have remained in the plumage are the grayish-brown eumelanins. In Cinnamon Cockatiels this has the effect of making the basic coloration appear gray-brownish, similar to that of the Cinnamon Zebra Finch. In combination with the yellow head and the red patches on the cheeks this looks very pleasing. This color variation is often found to be the winner at exhibitions these days.

Silver Cockatiels have red eyes and their

inheritance is recessive to the wild color. The overall color of the plumage is a pale silver to brownish-gray. They are considered difficult to breed because of a lethal factor which becomes apparent when they are mated among themselves.

It is highly unlikely that the mutative development of the

There is a mutation to suit almost any look desired by the hobbyists and breeders.

domesticated Cockatiel has been completed. We have been surprised by the different combinations which are possible. There appears to me to be scope for breeders, by means of selecting and combining, for the intensification of the yellow in the plumage of the Cockatiels. There are still far too few deep yellow birds, likewise golden "marked," cream-colored from silver x cinnamon, etc.

Even slate-black birds with olive-green spots have been cultivated. This optical impression is caused by the increased portions of yellow in the plumage of selectively bred wild-colored birds and is most noticeable in the Slate-Black Cockatiels which some aviculturists have produced by selectively breeding from Grays.

In 1978, Mr. Stueber, Jr. in Hessen found himself the owner of the first Whiteheads, a brand new West German mutation. Theoretically these are "blue" Cockatiels from whose plumage the yellow is absent, as in the blue Budgerigars and now in many other Parrots, too. Cockatiels, however, cannot look blue since the melanin of the wild bird contains very little yellow. Consequently they are pure gray in the dark areas of their plumage and white where the wild-colored birds show yellow

Cinnamon Cockatiels do not have black coloring in the plumage. Instead, they have a grayish brown color that mixes well with the yellow heads and orange cheek spots.

psittacin, hence the name "Whiteheads." This results in an entirely different overall optical impression, something completely unusual, and it points towards many new possibilities, i.e., the transmission of this absence of yellow to all existing Cockatiel varieties. However, since the "Whitehead" character is passed on recessively, this will take a little longer, because at least one intermediate generation is needed. Also, at the present time this Cockatiel mutation is still expensive.

Meanwhile, what are probably the most beautiful Cockatiels of all already exist: Pure Albinos, snow-white including the crests and with red eyes! That it might be possible to derive these from the Lutinos described earlier was obvious and Stueber, Jr. succeeded in doing so in 1980 (the cock he started off with was heterozygous for Ino in any case and the original hen was a Lutino). The first Albinos are said to have been of a somewhat weak constitution, but crossing with robust Lutinos—if necessary, with other colors as well—is likely to ensure that in the not too distant future Albinos and Whiteheads in other colors will be offered at prices the hobbyist can afford.

How Cockatiels Get on With Others

Despite being the size of a pigeon, the Cockatiel behaves towards small birds with exemplary good nature, which means it can suitably be kept in association with a colorful mixture of birds from all sorts of species. Thus one can also keep and propagate individual breeding pairs in aviaries, and the latter may be stocked with Budgerigars, or with Neophemas (Grass Parakeets), themselves peaceable, or even with the cantankerous Agapornids (Lovebirds), and, indeed, small species of Finches. They will content themselves with defending the heart of their breeding territory, i.e., the area immediately surrounding the nest box, by making those characteristic, curious threatening movements with the wings, but are unlikely to use their sharp beaks. On the contrary, they should

Opposite: Cockatiels are peaceable towards other birds, but remember that many other species, such as amazon parrots, may behave aggressively towards the Cockatiels.

not, as occasionally happens, allow themselves to be driven out of their nest box by a tenacious pair of Budgerigars or Agapornids. Where there is danger of this, it is better to prevent disaster by removing the mischief makers.

As regards the association with Waxbills and other small birds, it must be borne in mind that with its long, pointed wings and its quick

Below: Cockatiels are able to get along with many other kinds of animals. **Opposite:** If a few of your aviary inhabitants become troublemakers, it's better to separate them out than tempt danger.

movements in flight the slender Cockatiel reminds one of a hawk. All small birds have programmed into them a pattern of behavior which protects them from their natural enemies: as soon as they spot a hawk-like bird, they take off at breakneck speed and dive into the nearest cover. The first impression of a flying Cockatiel therefore, can cause a panic to break out among them which easily leads to fatal accidents resulting from the collision with hard objects. For this reason, small birds should first be gradually adapted to the sight of Cockatiels (for instance by being kept in adjacent enclosures) and subsequently will be associated with them at the same time.

Some aviculturists let several pairs of Cockatiels breed in one and the same good-sized aviary. While this would not succeed with any of the other species of Parakeets—with the exception of Budgerigars and some species of Lovebirds that breed in colonies—the Cockatiels may cope, provided they have an adequate number of nest boxes at their disposal (preferably twice as many as are normally supplied). Especially in the early stages, however, it must be anticipated that the pairs will disturb each

other, that there will be
fights between rival
cocks, etc., all of which
can ruin the breeding
results of some pairs or
at least detract from
them. Even if there are
plenty of nesting
facilities to choose
from, often several

If pairs of Cockatiels are kept in a colony, hens will sometimes lay eggs in a communal nest.

females are hell bent on breeding inside one and the same nest box, which generally bodes ill. For reasons of expediency alone, it is better, therefore, to provide for a separate enclosure compartment for each pair, perhaps by means of partitions inside the large aviary. Outside the breeding season, on the other hand, there need be no reservations about keeping Cockatiels of both sexes in larger groups (without nest boxes).

Index